Heiner Henninges/Bob Shell
Metz Flash Systems

Magic Lantern Guides
Proof of Purchase
Metz Flash
Systems

Heiner Henninges/Bob Shell

Flash Systems

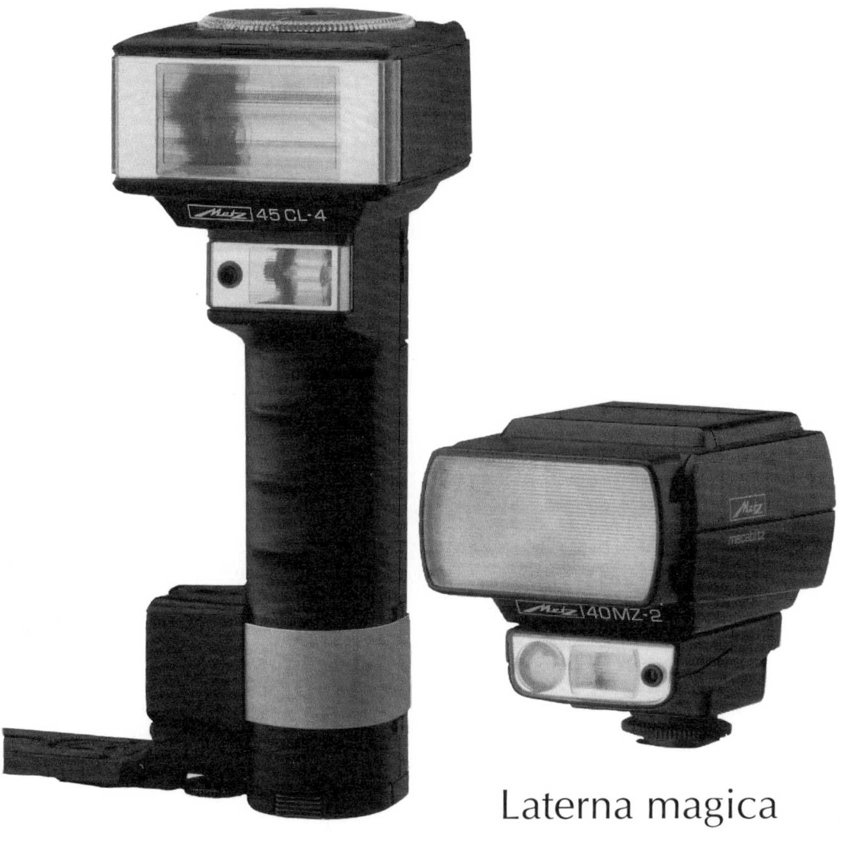

Laterna magica

Magic Lantern Guide to
Metz Flash System

A Laterna magica® book

First English Language Edition March 1994
Published in the United States of America by
Silver Pixel Press
Division of
The Saunders Group
21 Jet View Drive
Rochester, NY 14624

Based on the German edition by Heiner Henninges
Edited by Bob Shell
Translated by Phyllis M. Riefler-Bonham
Production Editor: Jerry O'Neill
Editorial Assistant: Mimi Netzel
Production Coordinator: Marti Saltzman

Printed in Germany by Kösel GmbH, Kempten

ISBN 1-883403-04-9

 The publisher acknowledges the assistance of Gary Barton and Robert Smythe of Daymen Photo Marketing, with thanks also to everyone at Bogen Photo for their patience and expertise.

Contents

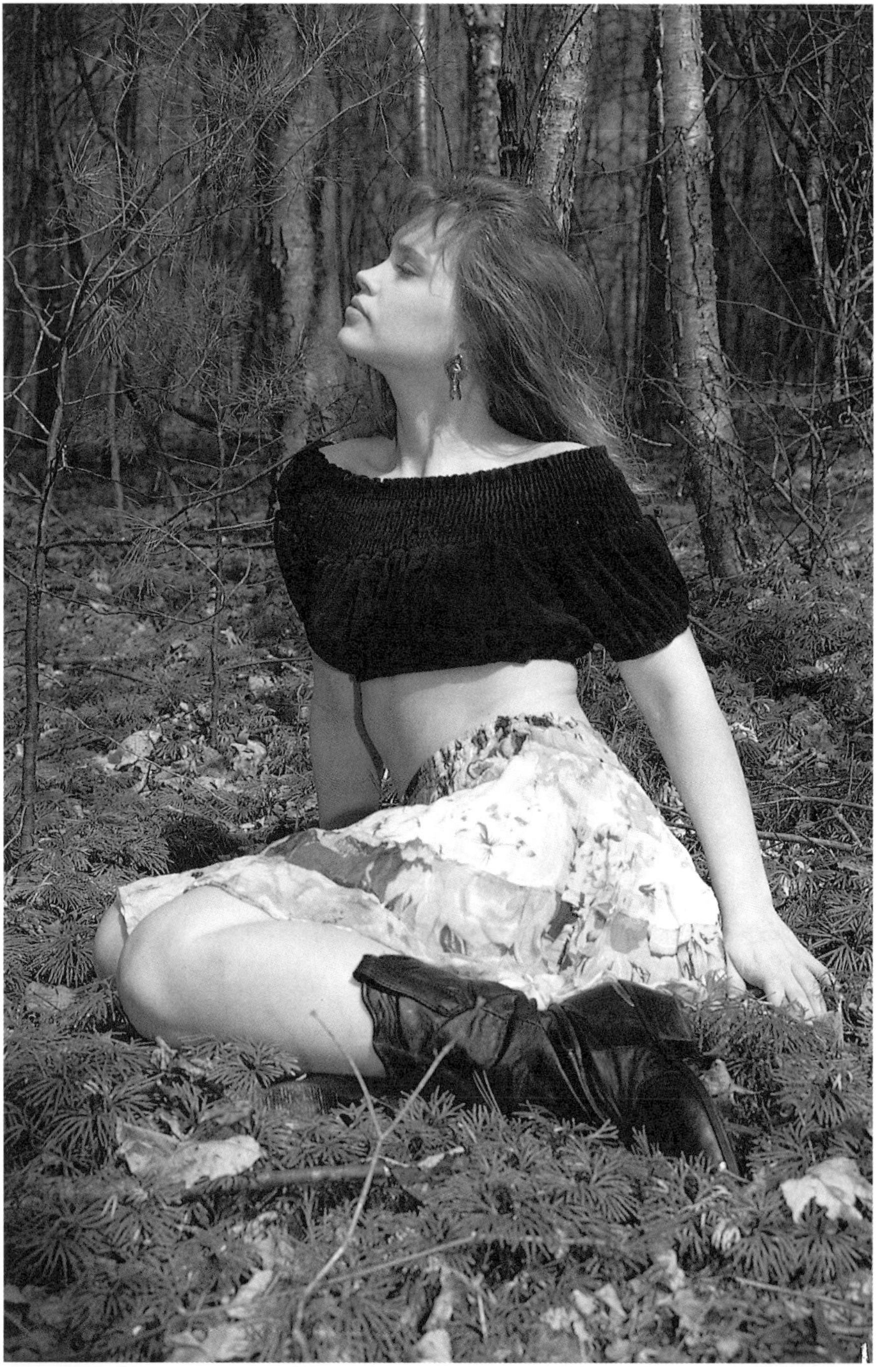

Basics of Flash Photography

Every photographer has seen pictures that freeze just the right moment. These pictures reveal in a flash what normally remains hidden from the human eye: the bullet passing through a playing card, the glass fragments of an exploding light bulb floating in space, or the splashing milk drop which raises a crown from the surface for a thousandth of a second after the impact.

Or a photograph may show a bee with such clarity that each tiny hair, though gigantic on the projection screen, is sharp and distinct. This picture could hardly be captured without the help of an electronic flash unit. Electronic flash can also impart a subtle translucence to a leaf, disclosing its structure, or it can momentarily reveal hidden subjects and otherwise imperceptible colors.

Electronic flash may be used almost anywhere. It is the photographer's personal sun, available no matter what the weather or lighting conditions. Photographers who use flash only when it is too dark for taking pictures miss a wealth of opportunities for enhancing their photos and expanding the variety of ways a subject can be captured on film.

Using flash poses no limits to creativity. If electronic flash is used with artistic as well as technical proficiency to strengthen composition and provide targeted illumination, almost all fields of photography will reveal new aspects. Even the most common features can be shown in a new light.

Flash can produce either super-sharp or blurred subjects, with either high or reduced contrast. Because flash light is balanced to resemble daylight, it does not produce a color cast on most commonly used films. Flash exposures are most impressive when the use of an electronic flash is hardly noticeable because it represents only part of the total exposure.

⇦ **Properly balanced fill flash will improve the lighting in a photograph without appearing unnatural. Here ambient light was measured first and then the flash exposure was reduced by 1-1/2 stops. Photo: Bob Shell.**

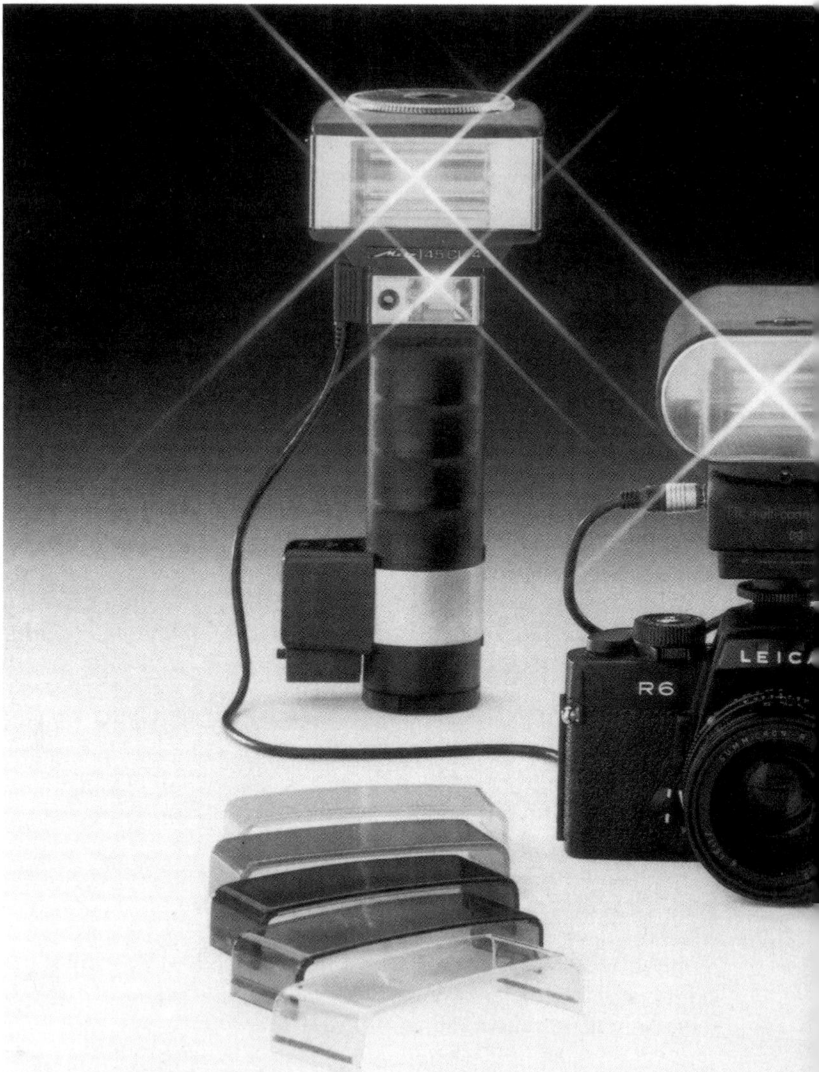

The Metz Flash System includes a wide range of accessories for professional flash applications. These include the TTL Multiconnector and SCA adaptors for integration with a camera's dedicated flash functions.

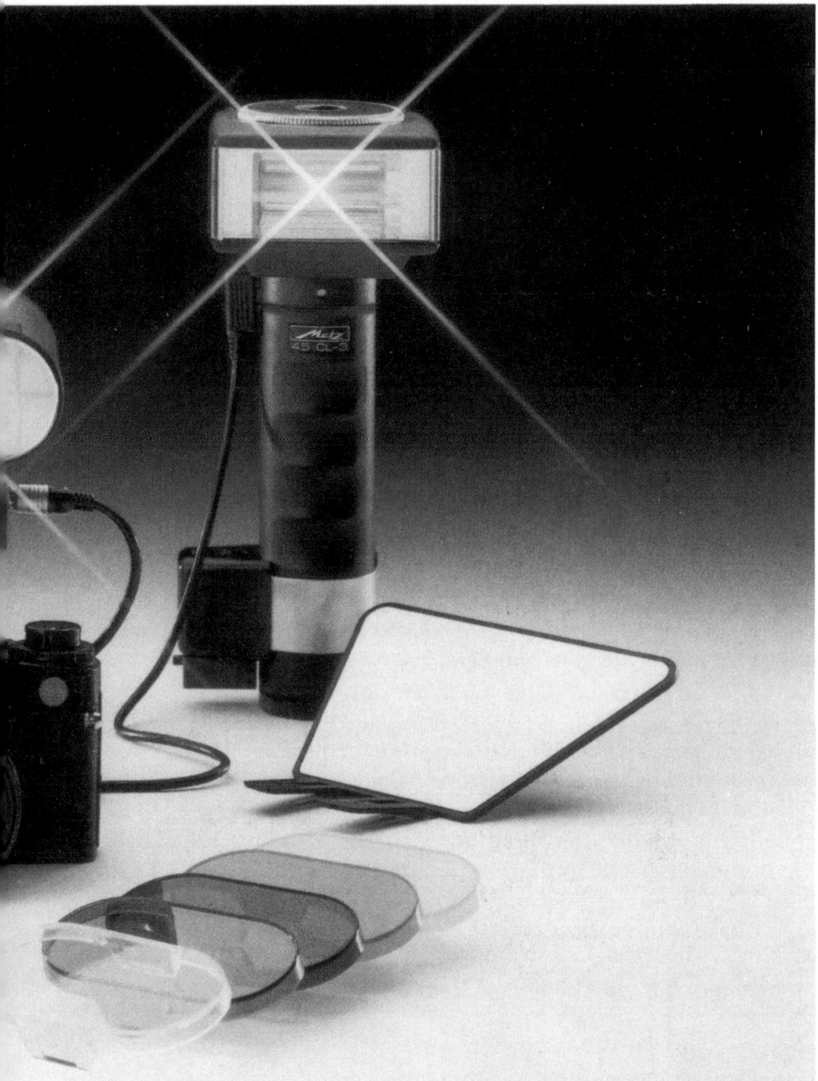

Accessory grips, color filters and reflectors for bounce flash offer numerous other options for advanced flash techniques.

Unfortunately, unimaginative use of flash has resulted in the widespread prejudice that the atmosphere of a situation is destroyed when flash pictures are taken. Therefore it is necessary to get acquainted with a few basics of flash technology which will help you understand flash photography and the special techniques that professionals use.

A careful study of this book will encourage the reader to use flash more frequently and will show that a touch of flash can enhance pictures in many situations. As a result, your pictures will improve technically as well as artistically. After you take even a few flash exposures using your new knowledge, you will see that lighting with flash can have many advantages.

Principles of Flash Illumination

Modern flash technology may be easier to grasp if you consider that there are actually only two ways to use flash.

Main light: The electronic flash unit provides all of the light for an exposure. This means that flash illumination is used to provide adequate lighting for the photograph.

Fill light: The electronic flash unit aids in the exposure and provides only part of the light used for an exposure. In this case the light from the flash complements, balances or enhances the existing lighting.

All other flash techniques, regardless of what they may be called, are only modifications of these two methods. All of them are designed to reduce the risk of faulty exposures. The term "fill flash" (or "fill-in flash") actually represents only one form of additional flash illumination. Beyond this, the basic concepts of flash which involve light energy, guide number, color temperature, etc. all play a part in the final outcome of the finished photograph.

Light Output

In flash photography the brightness of a subject is a function of the output of the flash unit and the resulting photographic exposure is a function of the duration of this output. Therefore, the actual light energy emitted by the flash is a product of the flash output and duration.

Brightness decreases with distance: Not only is the energy emitted by the flash unit important to the final exposure, but also the amount of energy that actually strikes the subject. Therefore, the distance of the flash unit from the subject is important. Almost all light sources emit light at a specific angle, or cone of illumination. The area covered by this cone increases with increasing distance. This means that the same brightness will be distributed over an increasingly larger area. Because of this, an object will receive less light the farther it is located from the source of the light. Thus, light from a flash unit is subject to the Inverse Square Law that brightness decreases in proportion to the square of the distance.

The effect of increased light on flash distance: Doubling the light increases the shooting range by only about 1-1/2 times. Therefore, if the flash provides correct exposure for a subject 10 feet away with the camera's lens set at an aperture of f/5.6, opening the lens to f/4 will provide correct exposure only as far as 14 feet, not 20 feet. Opening the aperture one stop allows twice as much light to pass, but the flash will only reach only 1.4 times as far. Again, this is determined by the Inverse Square Law.

Guide Number

The guide number is a value which quantifies the relationship between brightness, distance, and ISO film sensitivity. It has been defined to calculate the values which are important in practical applications, namely aperture and distance and is usually stated using ISO 100 film as the standard. With today's flash equipment, performing guide number computations is usually not necessary because the units are equipped with an f/stop scale, a computing dial, or an LCD display which indicates the aperture required for the distance, once the film's ISO speed has been set.

However, it is important to understand basic flash principles for use in situations where adjustments to the flash output are required. Even when using a camera with through-the-lens (TTL) flash metering adjustments to the flash exposure may occasionally be required.

Guide number, aperture, and distance: Guide numbers are designed to make it easy for the photographer to calculate the lens aperture needed for a flash exposure, and therefore guide numbers follow a logarithmic progression comparable to f/stops, but in reverse. (A numerically larger guide number means more light, while a numerically larger f/stop means less light.) For example, if the distance from the subject along with the guide number corresponding to the film sensitivity are known, the required aperture may be determined quite easily. This answers the question of what aperture to select to obtain the correct exposure for a subject at a given distance. Aperture = guide number/distance.

Note: *Since distance is part of the guide number formula, guide numbers are calculated in terms of meters or feet. In the United States, the stated guide number is calculated in feet and is consequently 3.3 times larger than the corresponding metric guide number. The main model number for Metz flash units is the actual metric guide number rating for the unit.*

Guide number with side lighting: The guide number computation will be accurate only when the camera lens and the flash are more or less aligned on a vertical axis — with an angle of not more than about 30 degrees separating them. For side lighting at angles greater than 30 degrees, compute the aperture in the usual way, and then make a correction by opening the lens to a wider f/stop. Open the aperture by:

- 1/2 f/stop at 45 degrees
- 1 f/stop at 60 degrees
- 2 f/stops at 70 degrees
- At an angle of 80 degrees, the flash is used strictly for effect and the exposure should not change by more than 1 f/stop from that required for the existing light or for the main flash.

Faster film speeds: Changing film speed also involves multiplying by 1.4. If you change to a faster film with twice the ISO speed, multiply the slower film's guide number by a factor of 1.4 to find the GN for the faster film. Or, if you change to a much faster film with four times the ISO speed, the guide number will be doubled.

Guide number and zoom flash heads: Typically, guide numbers are based on the image angle of a standard focal length lens; e.g. a 50mm lens on a 35mm camera. However, the guide number will change if the flash unit's angle of illumination is changed.

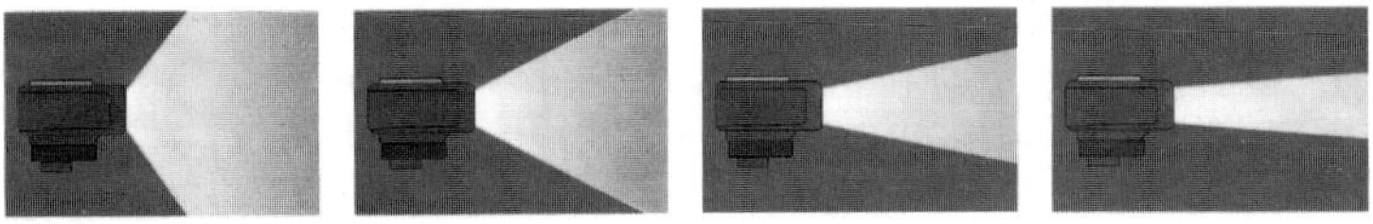

Metz flash units with zoom flash heads allow the angle of illumination to be adjusted to match the focal length of the lens in use. This provides optimum utilization of the light from the flash and makes the most of the available battery power.

With zoom flash heads the illumination angle is modified so that the angle of view of different focal lengths will be covered by the flash. This is accomplished by changing the position of the flash head diffuser in relation to the flash tube. By adjusting the zoom head, the flash energy is either concentrated on a smaller angle of illumination, hence greater distance, or diffused over a larger angle, hence shorter distance. The following applies: The smaller the angle of illumination (long focal lengths), the greater the guide number; the greater the angle of illumination (short focal lengths), the smaller the guide number. This explains why a flash unit — even though its flash tube always emits the same quantity of light — will have several different guide numbers when the reflector is adjusted to cover different angles. This is an important consideration because most professional flash units feature zoom heads which match the focal length of the lens being used.

Guide number in autoflash "Telecomputer" mode: In automatic flash modes the guide number of the flash corresponds to the maximum (or full) output when the flash is fired without automatic system compensation. If the subject or the distance requires less light from the flash, the duration of the flash is reduced by the autoflash system. Therefore, the automatic system saves you from having to make computations with guide numbers and apertures.

Other considerations: In addition to the factors above, a guide number applies to an average-size, average-brightness room. Therefore, it can only be used as a general guide. Knowing the guide number of a flash unit allows the photographer to estimate the maximum distance range of the flash unit and to make optimum use of the light it produces.

Color Temperature

The light from a Metz Mecablitz flash unit has a color temperature of 5600°K which approximates daylight. Thus, when using flash, daylight-balanced film should be used. This also makes flash an excellent source of light for augmenting ambient daylight or for use in fill flash photography.

Understanding Automatic Flash

In order to appreciate the limitations and advantages of different autoflash modes, it is helpful to understand how they work.

Flash Output Control

Principle: If the autoflash system determines the distance from the subject and the selected aperture before firing, it will simply adjust its output accordingly before firing. A flash with a guide number of 40, an aperture of 8, and a distance from the subject of 13 feet would automatically be adjusted downward to a guide number of 32, and at 10 feet to a guide number of 24, etc. Generally this is accomplished fairly simply; complex electronic control of the actual flash output is currently not used by any camera/autoflash system (instead they simply adjust the duration of the flash).

Aperture Selection with Flash

Film speed settings: In order for an automatic flash unit to determine the required flash output, the film speed being used must be set on the unit. With some cameras the film speed is relayed to the flash unit automatically, with other camera/flash combinations the film speed must be set manually.

Setting the aperture: There are two choices for setting the correct aperture, depending on the camera and flash being used. The lens can be set manually to the appropriate f/stop, or more advanced cameras will often set the correct f/stop automatically.

On the back of today's simpler flash units there is an adjustable slide or dial with one, two or three color codes, each corresponding to an f/stop. This dial is used to select an aperture, which is usually dependent on the required distance range, and the lens is then set to that f/stop. More elaborate flash units cover an entire spectrum of apertures, either indicated by an adjustment dial, as on the Metz handle mount flash units, or displayed digitally on an LCD display. The dial or display indicates the largest and smallest apertures available. This broad selection of f/stops is most advantageous when using fill flash.

Exposure verification: Each time the flash is fired, an LED on the flash unit indicates that the amount light produced by the flash resulted in a correct exposure .

Control of Flash Duration

Automatic "Telecomputer" Flash

Automatic flash is a relatively simple concept. A photocell or sensor on the flash unit detects the light that has been reflected off the subject. When the correct amount of light has been detected, the sensor system cuts off the flash. Metz calls this type of automatic sensor, flash output control, "telecomputer" flash.

Thyristor control: Most modern flash units avoid wasting energy by using a solid-state controller called a thyristor, which cuts off the flash while retaining the unused energy in the capacitor for the next flash. Therefore, the capacitor needs less energy to bring it back up to a full charge, so the flash unit recycles faster and allows faster consecutive flash exposures. In addition, thyristor-controlled flash units yield significantly more flashes per set of batteries. This state-of-the-art technology is available in most current electronic flash units.

IGBT advanced technology: Some of the newer, more sophisticated flash units, like the Metz Mecablitz 40 MZ 2, use an even more advanced electronic control system called an IGBT (Insulated Gate Bipolar Transistor). The IGBT system provides delay-free energizing or de-energizing and control of the flash, and requires about 30% fewer components. As a result, flash designers can add more features to a flash unit of the same size, or put the same features into a more compact unit.

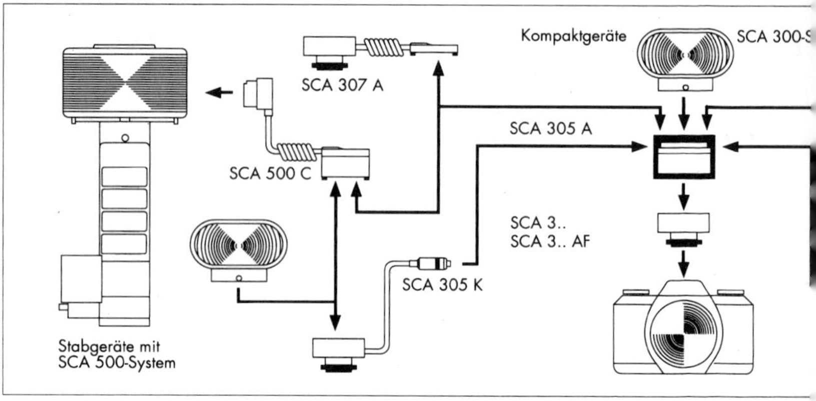

Advantages of automatic flash: As discussed, computing the correct aperture for flash pictures by using the guide number isn't quick nor is it always reliable. Automatic flash units simplify this process with exceptionally good results. Thus, when automatic flash units first appeared on the market, they were immediately well-received. Metz still offers this type of flash in its "telecomputer" line of flash units.

Flash Tips for Automatic "Telecomputer" Flash

Fill flash: The indicated f/stop for automatic flash applies to flash-only lighting. When using flash to fill-in existing lighting, one rule of thumb is to double the indicated f/stop. (If the indicated f/stop is f/4, for instance, set the lens to double the number, or f/8.) This reduces the flash output to two f/stops less than the existing light. Some professionals prefer to just go one f/stop higher which will give a more obvious fill flash effect. Whatever your preference, this is basically a simple yet effective method to compute fill-in flash exposure.

Variable aperture zooms: The effective aperture on some zoom lenses changes throughout the zoom range. This is usually indicated by labeling the lens with two apertures, such as f/3.5-4.5. Taking flash photos with this type of lens may require adjusting the aperture setting on the lens; consult the instructions provided with the lens.

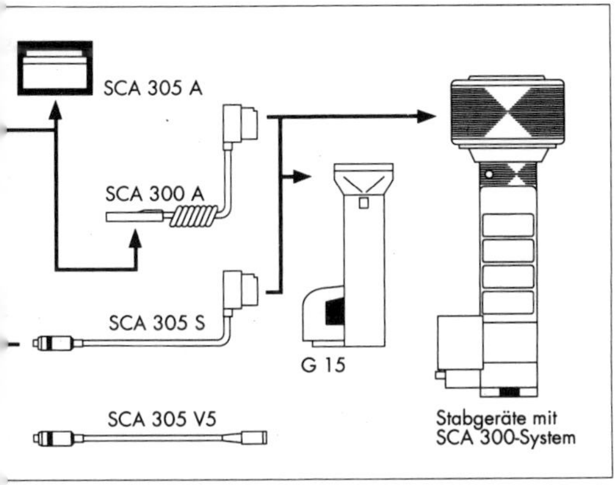

With the SCA Adapter System, the advantages of Metz professional flash units can be combined with a camera's sophisticated, dedicated flash functions. Lighting control with bounce or off-camera flash is easily achieved when the camera's TTL flash functions are used.

Standard TTL (Through-the-Lens) Flash

When using TTL autoflash, the flash exposure is measured through-the-lens (TTL) off the film plane (OTF). The mirror is flipped up, the aperture closes down to the correct value, the shutter curtain opens fully, and then the flash is fired. During the period when the shutter is open, the flash metering cell (usually on the bottom or side of the camera's mirror box) measures the light reflected off the film and regulates the flash duration as a result of this reading.

Advantages of TTL Flash

Compared with conventional, non-TTL automatic flash, TTL flash control has the advantage that it covers the image angle of the subject accurately. Since only the light which actually reaches the film is measured, light loss caused by lens attachments such as teleconverters, extension tubes or filters are also automatically taken into consideration. Even zoom lenses that change their effective aperture when zoomed to different focal lengths (variable aperture zooms) do not present a problem with TTL flash measurement.

Unlimited aperture selection with TTL: TTL flash metering also allows you to utilize any f/stop with flash, while automatic flash control that uses a sensor on the flash unit generally permits using only a given selection of two or three f/stops. (Metz handle-mount flash units and top-of-the-line Metz compact flash units are an exception because they offer a large number of aperture settings.) With TTL flash you can select the optimum depth of field or pick an exact combination of shutter speed and aperture

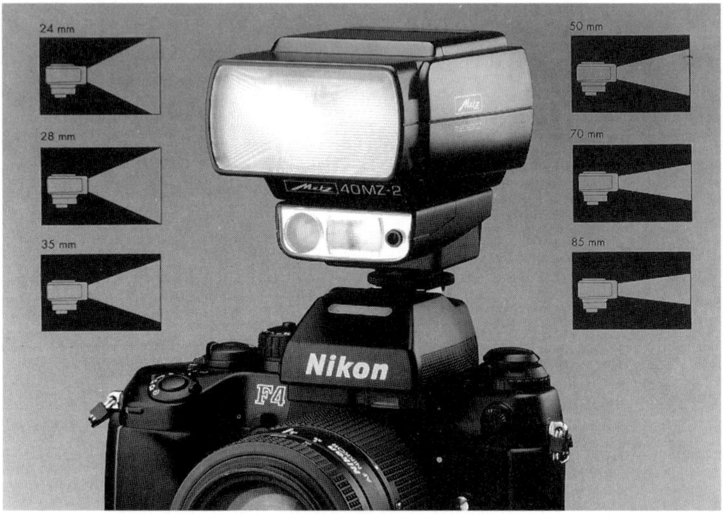

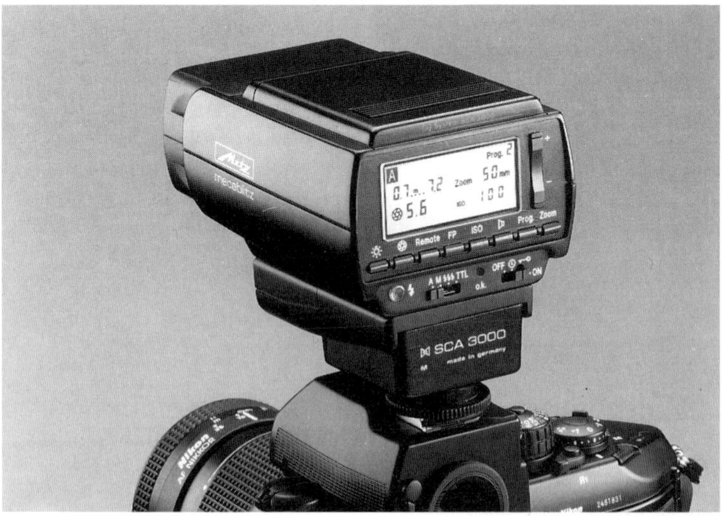

when shooting with fill flash or mixed light. The ability to make a precise choice from all the aperture values expands the working range of your flash, not only the maximum shooting ranges.

Ideal with mixed lighting: TTL metering can make it easier to expose for difficult lighting situations. Because the camera's sophisticated metering measures both flash and existing light, you'll even find it easy to make mixed-light exposures that combine ambient light with flash. Fill flash exposures can be handled automatically. In addition, TTL flash makes it relatively simple to use several flash units simultaneously, with a central automatic control.

Limitations of Standard TTL Autoflash

If the main subject does not fill the picture and is not at a uniform distance, only a fraction of the light from the flash will be reflected by the subject. The remainder of the light emitted by the flash is lost in the background "next to" the main subject. The TTL autoflash attempts to overcome this by prolonging the duration of the flash. The result is overexposed main subjects, if there is substantial separation between the subject and the background.

Unusual reflectance of the subject: Problems arise with subjects exhibiting a greater or lesser degree of reflectance than average. Autoflash is calibrated (as are most exposure meters) for a subject with medium reflectance. This calibration to so-called, "18% or medium gray" may have a negative effect on flash metering and control. Naturally dark subjects with low reflecting power will be lightened automatically and reproduced in an unnaturally light manner. Conversely, very light subjects with high reflecting power will be photographed in an unnaturally dark manner. The bride in white in front of the white wall will be too dark, the

The Metz Mecablitz 40 MZ 2 is a powerful, sophisticated flash unit. Thanks to the SCA 3000 System it can master every flash mode from manual to automatic, including TTL and cordless TTL flash metering. Depending on the camera, the zoom reflector's coverage can be automatically adjusted to match the focal length of the lens in use. This information is relayed to the photographer by the flash unit's liquid crystal display (LCD) readout.

black cat in front of the black car will be too light. If you want to do better than the autoflash, you must set the flash unit and the camera to manual flash mode. If the subject reflects light in a highly irregular manner, you should not rely on any form of automatic flash. In these types of situations many photographers use fully manual flash calculated with a handheld flash meter.

Corrections are also often needed with mixed-light exposures when the subject exposed by the flash has a much different reflectance than the rest of the photograph, or when a very small amount of flash illumination is used and is difficult to control with sufficient accuracy. Also it may be necessary to make exposure corrections when the subject is not in the center of the picture.

Note, if using Polaroid test exposures with TTL flash: *The reflectance characteristics of Polaroid instant slide film emulsions are different from conventional films. This calls for exposure compensation because most TTL metering systems read the light reflected from the film surface. This should be considered if predetermining exposures for conventional film.*

Simple TTL Auto Fill flash

This automatic feature, offered by many cameras and available with the SCA dedicated system, makes an automatic preflash correction but may still require adjustment for ambient light or background brightness.

Exposure metering in TTL flash affects only ambient light: The automatic flash features of most current cameras work with a selected camera exposure metering method. This affects only the measurement of ambient light. TTL flash control is completely independent of this. Some cameras with auto fill flash also have an automatic minus correction of the flash exposure; this automatically counteracts overexposure of the foreground.

Limits of conventional TTL auto fill flash: When there is a noticeable amount of ambient light or the subject is definitely backlit, existing light and/or background brightness must be exposed with an appropriate combination of shutter speed and aperture for natural-looking results. This does not necessarily occur automatically with conventional TTL auto fill flash.

Flash Synchronization

For proper results, the electronic flash must fire when the shutter is completely open. If the camera has a between-the-lens or leaf shutter, as found in many medium and large format lenses, the photographer may use very fast shutter speeds for flash photography. The design of these shutters allows them to be completely open in a very short amount of time thus, flash synchronization is less complicated.

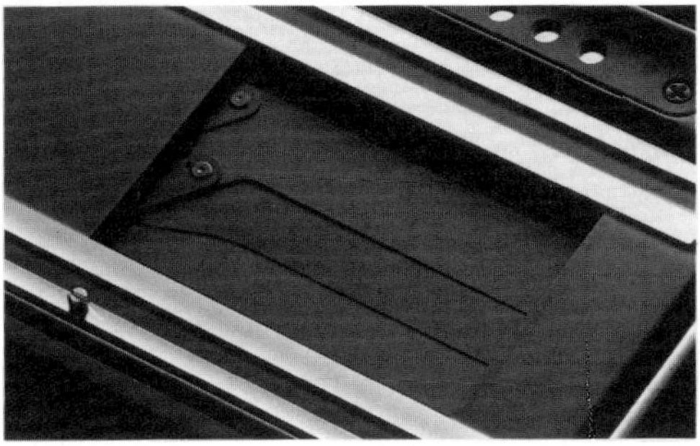

For proper exposure, the flash must be fired when the focal plane shutter is completely open across the entire film frame. Thus, cameras with focal plane shutters have a maximum synchronization speed. Using a faster shutter speed will cause a portion of the film to be unexposed.

Focal plane shutters: Flash synchronization is more complicated when using cameras with focal plane shutters, such as nearly all 35mm SLR cameras. A focal plane shutter consists of two curtains which move in sequence across the film. The first curtain opens, uncovering the film for exposure, and then the second curtain closes providing a light-tight cover over the film again. Both curtains move at a constant speed in most shutter designs. Exposure time is changed by increasing or decreasing the amount of time before the second curtain is released. In this case the synchronization speed is critical because the flash can only be synchronized at shutter speeds in which the shutter is fully open.

Thus, the fastest synchronization speed for electronic flash is the highest shutter speed at which the first curtain has completely uncovered the film and the second has not yet begun to close. The synchronization speed only indicates the highest possible shutter speed for a flash exposure. Most cameras also allow the photographer to set slower shutter speeds for use with flash.

Shutters moving horizontally (along the longer side of the film) usually use 1/60 second as the highest synchronization speed for electronic flash. In many modern cameras, the shutter curtains are made of titanium foil or other modern materials, rather than cloth, and move vertically (along the shorter film axis). This allows the curtain movement, and therefore the fastest synchronization speed, to be dramatically increased.

The difference between a synchronization speed of 1/60 second and 1/250 second becomes important when the amount of ambient light, at the selected shutter speed, is within approximately one f/stop of the flash exposure. In these cases the existing light should be included when computing the total exposure. A separate chapter is dedicated to useful combinations of flash with daylight or other existing light, so this will not be discussed further at this point. However, it is important to remember: The faster the flash synchronization speed offered by the camera, the easier it is to use flash modes such as fill flash.

Finally, we should note what happens when a camera with a focal plane shutter is set at a speed higher than the fastest synchronization speed. In this case only a portion of the normal image area is exposed. The remainder of the film area, which was still covered by the curtains during the flash, is severely underexposed. Modern cameras will automatically prevent this error. They simply refuse to fire a flash at too high a speed, and automatically default to the highest possible synchronization speed.

Note: *On some cameras, synchronization is given as X-time. With an X-setting, the flash is fired the instant that the shutter is fully open. Two other modes which are found on older cameras and shutters are M and FP. They are designed for use with old-fashioned flash bulbs. In these two cases the flash is fired approximately 20 or 30 milliseconds before the shutter opens, because flash bulbs require this much time to reach their maximum brightness. If an electronic flash is connected to an M or FP contact, the flash exposure will be completed before the shutter opens. The result will be severe underexposure, either a completely black transparency or a totally clear negative.*

Duration of electronic flash: The short flash duration of an electronic flash results in sharper handheld pictures and also freezes the subject's motion. It is not the camera's shutter speed but the duration of the flash that determines the exposure time for a photo lit entirely by flash. Therefore, when photographing in a darkened room, it makes no difference what shutter speed is used as long as the flash synchronization is maintained.

Flash synchronization with ambient light: The situation is different when photographing outside in daylight. The more ambient light there is, the greater its effect on the total exposure. When making a flash photograph in a situation where there is a significant amount of ambient light, using a slow shutter speed allows a greater amount of exposure by the existing light. Therefore, to prevent overexposure or motion blurs due to the ambient light, you must use the fastest possible shutter speed. A good rule to remember in these situations is that the aperture setting controls the flash exposure while the shutter speed setting controls the ambient light exposure.

Slow-synchronization: It used to be that flash release was not recommended with slower shutter speeds. This frequently caused double exposures due to the short-term flash and the additional long-term ambient light exposure. Any movement resulted in a blurred image superimposed on the sharp flash image. Usually this is considered unappealing, and only occasionally, "artistic." However, it is possible to place a non-moving main subject exposed with flash in front of a properly exposed existing light background if the shutter speed is selected carefully. At normal shutter speeds this would be a black background. This is why some newer cameras feature an automatic slow-sync function which allows the use of shutter speeds up to 30 seconds in all automatic flash modes. Other cameras permit the preselection of slower shutter speeds by combining TTL fill flash with manual exposure adjustment.

Rear curtain or second shutter sync: With normal synchronization, the flash is fired precisely after the opening of the first shutter curtain. This causes any exposure by ambient light to occur after the flash has fired. With rear curtain sync, however, the flash is triggered just before the second curtain begins to close, and the existing light exposure takes place before the flash is fired. The difference can be seen when photographing moving objects; they will have natural-looking motion blurs only with second curtain sync. This is a feature offered with many of today's professional cameras and is compatible with the Metz SCA dedication systems. (See also, SCA Adapter System Control Options, page 44.)

Other Flash Considerations

Covering a Range of Distances with Flash

With flash illumination, the selected aperture gives truly correct exposure for only one distance. Everything closer than that is overexposed, and everything farther away is underexposed. Making a successful flash picture of a large subject that covers a range of distances, for example eight friends around a banquet table, can only be done if you have a basic knowledge of flash characteristics.

Large groups: Let's look at an example. The first person at the table is 15 feet from the flash, requiring a flash unit with a guide number of 120 and an aperture of f/8. Another person, at a distance of 21 feet, should be taken at f/5.6 (guide number 120/21 feet = f/5.6), but since the photograph will be taken at f/8, the second person will be underexposed by one full stop. And a closer person, 11 feet from the camera, should get an exposure of f/11 (guide number 120/11 feet = 11), so at f/8 he will be overexposed by a full stop.

Close distances: At close distances these values are even more dramatic. A distance of 7.5 feet would require an aperture of f/16. A person 6 feet farther away, 13.5 feet from the camera, would require f/8. However, a difference of two f/stops is too great for most films to handle.

Increasing subject-to-flash distance: A mathematical operation shows one way out of this dilemma. Increasing the flash-to-subject distance minimizes the relative difference in distance between the closest and farthest subjects and therefore decreases the front-to-back brightness gradient in the picture, making the difference less critical. When you're photographing this kind of subject, take advantage of this "tele" effect as much as possible to even-out the illumination with flash.

Luckily, shooting from greater distances is possible with today's high-output flash units. These units are by no means a luxury or useful only to professionals; they are equally valuable for the serious amateur photographer. Their higher guide number allows a greater flash-to-subject distance and therefore more evenly illuminated pictures. Depending on the room's conditions, you can also lengthen the path of the flash light without moving farther from the subject by using indirect (bounce) flash.

Avoiding the Harshness of Direct Flash

The fact that flash is a directed source of light not only poses the problem of lighting the picture evenly, it also means that the light of electronic flash is rather harsh. This effect is intensified when the flash unit is mounted directly in the camera's hot shoe, since the light from the flash is almost parallel to the optical axis.

Front lighting: This type of lighting is called front lighting. It is not very suitable for three-dimensional subjects because it flattens them and they lose their depth. In addition, front lighting often casts disruptive shadows which are obvious if the subject is relatively close to a lighter background.

Shadows are also created when the flash unit is located to the side of the camera and lens; this occurs when a handle-mount flash unit is used with a simple bracket. This moderate side-lighting brings out the three-dimensional quality of the subject but is still very direct and often harsh.

Bounce flash: Flash lighting becomes aesthetically pleasing only when its harshness is reduced, which can often be accomplished by using bounce lighting. Bounce lighting is achieved by aiming the flash towards a white ceiling, wall or other large surface which causes the light to be reflected downward or sideways towards the subject. With this indirect lighting, the subject receives softer light and the shadows are less distracting. Furthermore, bounce flash prevents "red-eye" in portraits. Bounce lighting does have drawbacks, however. Bounce lighting requires increased output from the flash for proper exposure because the light must travel further and is more diffused. Another problem

The swivel/tilt head of a Metz handle-mount unit may be adjusted vertically by 90° and horizontally by 360°.

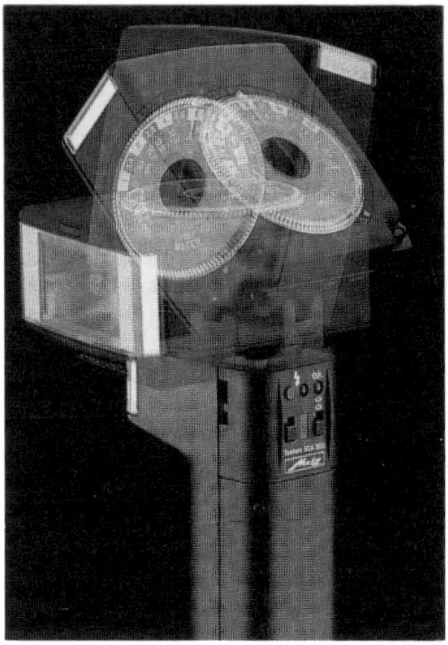

with bounce flash is that unless the surface the light bounces off is a neutral white, an unpleasant color cast may result.

Diffusers and reflectors: A reflector or diffusion panel, attached to the flash head, reduces the harshness of direct flash while eliminating the problems of color cast and lack of appropriate surfaces to bounce light off. There are dozens of styles of reflectors and diffusers, from a simple white card to more elaborate softboxes and umbrellas. The larger the reflector, the softer the light. Like bounce lighting however, diffusers spread the light over a larger area. Since less of the light is falling on the subject, flash output needs to be increased proportionately to compensate.

Other options: You can also use any of the lighting ideas described here for combinations of flash and existing light. When used together with existing light, "flash on camera" becomes much more pleasing, since it does not create such unpleasant shadows. Thus, if you are using equipment that requires mounting the flash unit in the camera's flash shoe, you should avoid flash-only exposures as much as possible. Instead, for better photos, use techniques that combine flash with the existing light. With a little bit of experience (and sometimes a monopod or tri-

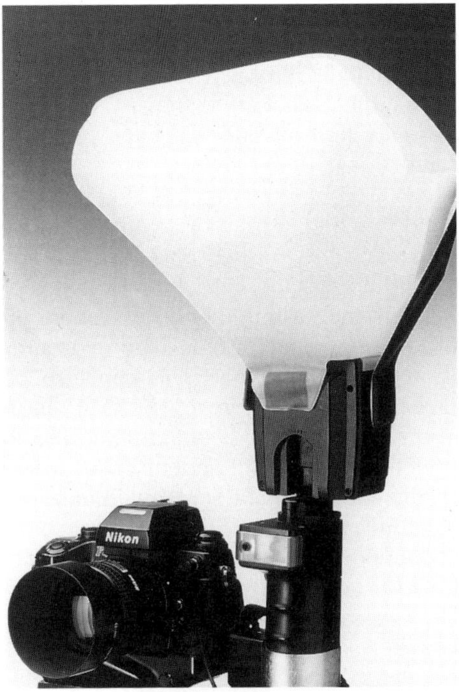

The Lumiquest® "Big Bounce" is fastened with Velcro™ strips to the flash head. Although it absorbs up to three f/stops of light, it softens the effect of the flash because it acts as reflector and mini-diffusion box.

pod), you won't have problems even when using relatively long exposure times of 1/30 or 1/15 second. Naturally, because it permits faster shutter speeds in existing light, a fast lens offers the greatest flexibility when mixing existing light with flash.

Using a faster film with flash illumination to convey a more desirable mood is also an option. In the past, this sometimes created problems because of the fast films' coarser grain and weaker colors. However the remarkable improvements in film technology in the past few years have made faster films more of an option, even in professional work. In most cases when recording an event or conveying a mood, using an ISO 200 or 400 color negative film and mixed lighting with flash is preferable to using a slower film and flash-only illumination. However, for the stringent demands of high-quality printed reproduction (magazine advertisements, for example) using a slow film and controlled lighting usually is still preferable.

Compensating for Light and Dark Subjects

The flash unit's measurement system assumes that the subject reflects an average amount of light. Problems may arise when flash exposures are taken of subjects that are extremely reflective or non-reflective. For unusually light or dark subjects, you may need to make exposure corrections.

Flash compensation: A child in white in front of a white wall, for example, will appear too dark in the finished photo, or a black dog sitting on a dark sofa will appear too light. In these types of situations, one solution is to set the flash unit and the camera on manual flash mode. After taking a series of bracketed exposures you should have at least one excellent shot. This can also be done in TTL, using exposure compensation to "bracket" flash duration by shifting from an assumed middle-value exposure to "overexpose" a highly reflective subject or "underexpose" a less reflective subject. This has the added benefit of maintaining a single working aperture, thus consistent depth of field.

Similar situations can happen in the close-up range, where the subject might be a white rose against a dark background or a dark-red rose against a light background.

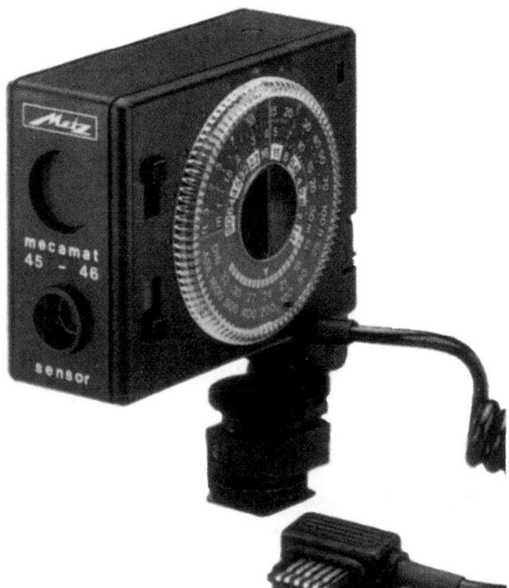

The Metz Mecamat 45-46 Sensor is recommended for accurate spot metering at close distances or when a particular exposure is necessary for fast moving objects.

This problem can also arise when taking flash pictures outdoors or when the background is far behind the subject. In these cases, the distant background will absorb light and should be treated as if it were a dark area. Otherwise the flash unit will increase its output to reach a "correct" exposure, but because of the dark background, the main subject will be overexposed. Typical examples are photographing people dancing in a large ballroom, or outdoors at a barbecue or garden party.

Metz Mecamat sensor: In cases like these, if using non-TTL automatic flash instead of making exposure corrections, you can change the measurement technique by using an external Metz Mecamat sensor. It measures an angle that is twice as narrow as the regular sensor. The Mecamat sensor also has a viewfinder, allowing you to align the measurement area with the most important part of the subject.

External sensor: By far the greatest problem with automatic (non-TTL) flash exposure control arises from the fixed angle covered by the flash unit's photocell which is usually 30 degrees. If the flash is used off-camera, some distance away from the camera, the photocell is measuring the light reflected back in the direction of the flash rather than the light reflected back to the camera lens. To prevent this discrepancy, an external sensor can be used at the camera position. The reading from the camera position also provides the starting point for making all manual corrections as discussed in conjunction with the guide number and listed in tables at the end of this book.

Wireless Control of Multiple Flash

Using a flash unit mounted directly on the camera often creates hard, unpleasant shadows in the picture, but this effect can be prevented by using one or more additional flash units. The simplest way to use multiple flash, without requiring inconvenient connecting wires between them, is to use photo slave releases and wireless or remote control systems. Both infrared (IR) and radio remote control systems are available.

The simplest units are photo slave releases that plug into the

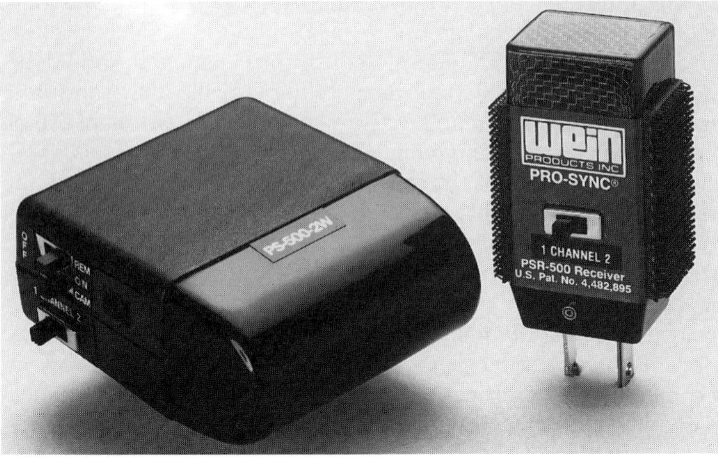

Wein Products, a leading manufacturer of remote release systems, has developed infrared-based systems that avoid the risk of electrical interference from cordless telephones, microphones, etc., that can disrupt radio control systems. The Wein Pro-Sync 500 Series uses coded pulses of infrared light for firing flash units at distances as far as 600 feet. The flash unit fires when the small batteryless receiver connected to it detects the infrared pulses.

off-camera flash units. When they are triggered by the pulse of light from the on-camera flash, they fire the flash unit(s) they are connected to. Units like the Mecalux are available from Metz and other suppliers. They are inexpensive and can be adapted to diverse applications.

More powerful remote control systems use transmitters and receivers for firing the off-camera flashes. The transmitter is fired by the camera's sync connection and sends an infrared or radio signal that triggers the receiver. The transmitter is small enough to fit easily on a standard flash bracket along with the camera and the flash unit.

The advantages of a multiple-channel system include controlling several flashes independently, whereas using a photocell system fires all slave flash units at the same time. Multiple-channel controls also prevent your remote flash units from being triggered by other photographers' flashes, important in situations such as wedding, news, and sports photography.

A flash unit that offers exceptional performance when used with a remote control is the Metz Mecablitz 60 CT 4. This compact, powerful and portable flash can conveniently be used off-camera, mounted on a light stand with an umbrella or reflector, to provide studio-type lighting on location. When used with a remote control, the battery-powered 60 CT 4 can be operated without the hazard of sync and power cables on the floor.

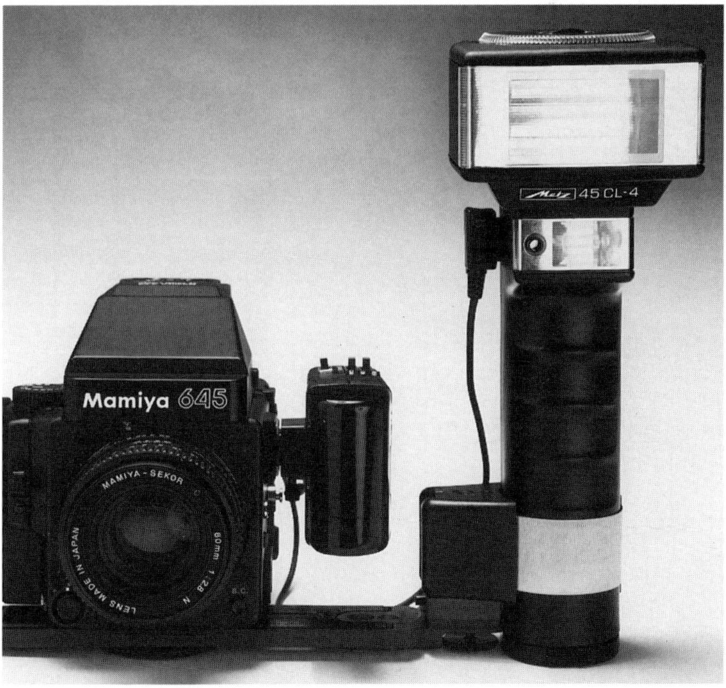

The Wein Pro-Sync infrared transmitter (pictured), makes it possible to fire a flash at the camera position as well as an unlimited number of remote flash units equipped with Pro-Sync receivers.

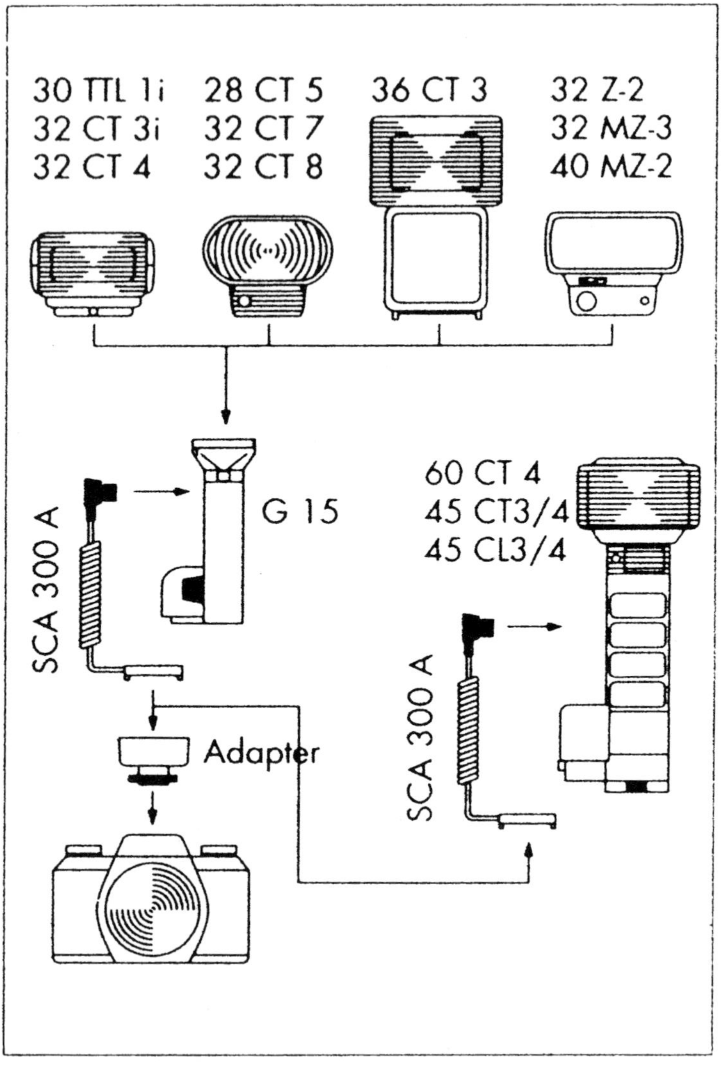

To maintain dedicated flash features with a handle-mount flash unit or Power Grip, connect the flash to a SCA 300 series adaptor with the SCA 300 A cord. The SCA 3000 A cord is available for use SCA 3000 series adaptors.

Using The SCA System

Almost all manufacturers of SLR (single lens reflex) cameras offer flash units as part of their system approach to automatic photography. These flash units are designed for specific cameras, allowing camera-specific dedication of many automatic flash functions. The flash and camera communicate to each other allowing sophisticated TTL program functions along with distance, focal length and aperture information. Some cameras allow the photographer to see critical flash information displayed in the camera's viewfinder, without removing their eye from the viewfinder to look at a display on the flash unit.

The special flash features available today could hardly have been envisioned by camera designers fifteen years ago, let alone by photographers. Previously, there had been attempts to equip flash units and cameras with a few specially coordinated functions, but these ideas were not met with enthusiasm by either users or flash equipment manufacturers. Photographers had to buy a different flash unit when changing to another camera, and flash manufacturers could not produce large, cost-effective pro-

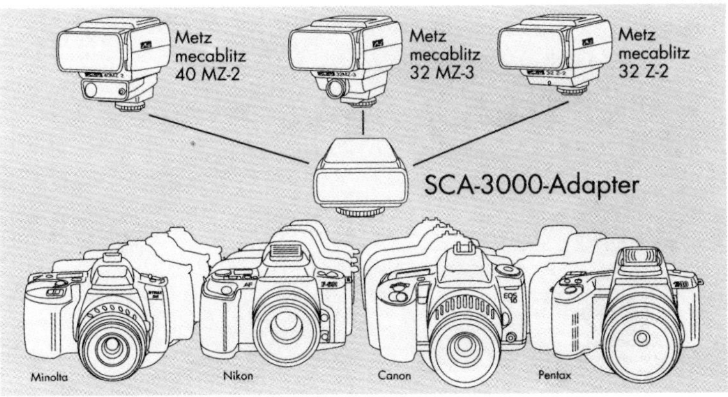

The new SCA 3000 System is designed for compatibility with the highly sophisticated TTL dedicated flash systems available with current Minolta, Nikon, Canon and Pentax AF cameras.

duction runs because each camera system required special connectors.

Independent flash unit manufacturers like Metz, however, could offer a more extensive assortment of flash units to meet the varied demands of advanced amateur and professional photographers. Over a period of 30 years, Metz has acquired considerable experience in developing flash units. Metz has shipped more than 10,000,000 flash units from the company's factory in Germany, to every part of the world, and Metz' market share in the handle-mount flash unit category exceeds 90%.

Increased Versatility with the SCA System

The Metz SCA (Special Camera Adaptation) system allows the use of flash units from your camera's manufacturer as well as Metz flash units, thereby providing photographers with great flexibility. By using different adapters for different camera systems, a photographer can use the same SCA-compatible flash unit on several different cameras. Therefore, the camera may change but the flash remains the same. Special functions which can be utilized with a given camera, flash and adaptor system will be listed at the end of the chapter discussing the respective techniques.

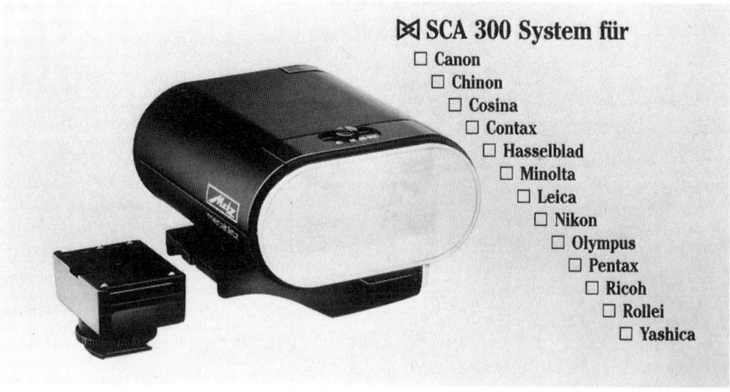

By using SCA System Adapters, Metz Mecablitz shoe mount flash units (models 28 and above) will be compatible with the dedicated flash systems of modern SLR cameras. The appropriate adapter is inserted in the laterally-rotating foot of the Mecablitz flash unit.

The SCA adapter combines the flash unit and the camera into one integral unit, offering all of the dedicated features available for that camera system. SCA adapter systems are available for 35mm SLR cameras, including Canon, Contax, Leica, Minolta, Nikon, Pentax and Yashica. When a medium format is desirable, Bronica, Rollei and Hasselblad allow the automatic control of Metz Mecablitz flash units with the use of the SCA adapter system. But even photographers who use a camera that does not support dedicated flash functions can utilize flash technology. Only a few manual adjustments are required.

The SCA 300 System for Analog Control

As early as 1980, engineers at Metz-Werke GmbH & Co. KG (the company's official name) succeeded in adapting Metz flash units to existing cameras, utilizing all the special flash functions known at that time. They solved the problem of handling the many different types of connectors, varying control systems, and special camera and flash functions provided by different manufacturers by designing a relatively uncomplicated adapter, the SCA 500 system. But the SCA 500 system was not the end. The SCA 300 system followed very soon thereafter, providing diverse functions and controls simply by sliding the appropriate flash adapter foot into the camera's hot shoe. Contained in the adapter foot is the interface for all flash functions.

The SCA adapter system was soon adopted by many other flash unit manufacturers. If you wish to purchase SCA adapters, see your Metz dealer. Currently, SCA units for 35mm cameras are distributed to photographic dealers in the US by Bogen Photo and in Canada by Daymen Photo Marketing Ltd. Medium format adapters are available through the distributor for a particular medium format camera.

SCA adapters can control special flash functions for more than 250 different types of cameras. These adapters are manufactured by Metz and meet demanding requirements. Flash control systems are technically complex, must perform to very high standards, and require fitting many complex components into the extremely small space inside the adapter foot. Tiny microchips, assembled by Metz, often operate on several levels.

SCA 300 summary of functions

AV-1/AL-1		●	●					
AT-1			●					
T 50/T 70/T 80		●	●		●			
T 90		●	●		●	●		
1000 FN/EOS620/650/ 1000/1000F		●	●			●		□
EOS Rebel/Rebel S		●	●			●		□
EOS 1/600/RT		●	●			●		□
EOS 10/100/ELAN		●	●			●		○
EOS 700/750/850			●			●		□
EOS 600/620/650	312	●	●			●		●
1000 FN/EOS 1/RT/ 1000/1000F	AF	●	●			●		●
EOS Rebel/Rebel S		●	●			●		●
EOS 10	312/2	●	●			●		○
EOS 700/750/850	AF		●			●		●
EOS 100/ELAN		●	●			●		●
CONTAX								
MD 137/139/RTS II	380	●	●	●		●		
MA 137/159 MM/ 167 MT7)		●	●	●		●		
RTS III7)		●	●	●		●		
COSINA								
CT-3/CT-4/CT-7/CT-10	360	●	●					
CT-20/CS-2/CS-3		●	●					
HASSELBLAD								
500 ELX/503 CX/553 ELX	390 1)	●		●		●		
205 TCC		●		●		●		
LEICA								
R 4/R 4S	351	●	●	●				
R 5/R-E		●	●	●		●		
R 6/R 6-2		●		●		●		
R 7		●	●	●		●		

mecablitz 28 CT..+G15, 30 TTL1+G15, 32 CT..+G15, 36 CT..+G15, 45 CT 3/4, 45 CL 3/4, 60 CT 4 (with F3)	344	●	●	●		●		

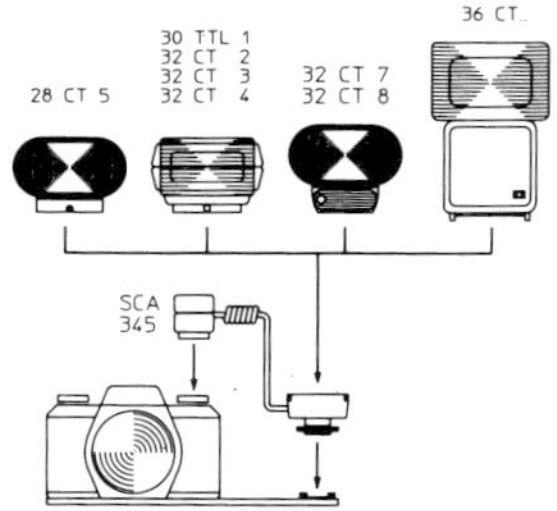

mecablitz 28 CT../ 30 TTL 1/ 32 CT../ 36 CT.. (with F3)	345	●	●	●		●		
FE/EM/FG-20	346 AF	●	●	●				
FM-2	346/2	●		●				
FE-2/FA/FG/F 601M	AF	●	●	●		●		
F 301/N 2000/N 6000		●	●	●		●		
F 401/F 501		●	●	●		●		●
F 801 3)/F 801s 3)		●	●	●		●		●
N 4004/N 2020/N 8008 3)		●	●	●		●		●
F 401s/F 401x 2/3)		●	●	●		●		●
F 4 3)/F 4s 3)		●	●	●		●		●
F 601 2/3)/N 6006 2/3)		●	●	●		●		●
OLYMPUS								
OM-1 N	321	●		●				
OM-10/OM-10 Quartz/		●	●	●				
OM-20/OM-G/OM 30		●	●	●				
OM-F	321	●	●	●				
OM-2 N/OM-4/		●	●	●		●	●	

ME-Super/ME-F/MG	Cord A 1) 4P Synch-Cord B	●	●					
MV/MV-1		●	●	●				
Super-A/645		●	●	●	□	●	●	
Program A/A 3/A 3000		●	●	●	□			
SFX/SF1		●	●	□		●	●	□
$SFX_N/SF1_N$/SF7/SF10		●	●	□			●	□
P 30/P 30 N/P 3 N		●	●	●	□			
P 30T/P 50		●	●	●	□			
SFX/SF1	374/2 AF	●	●	●		●	●	●
$SFX_N/SF1_N$/SF7/SF10		●	●	●		●		●
Z1 2)/Z10 2)/PZ10 2)		●	●	●		●		●
PRAKTICA								
BMS	321	●		●				
BC 1/BCA		●	●	●				
BX 20		●	●	●		●		
RICOH								
XR-1S/KR-5S	364	●						
XR-2S/XR-S/XR-F		●	●					
XR-7/XR-6/XR -20 SP		●	●					
KR-10/KR-10S/KR-30 SP		●	●					
KR 10 M		●	●					
XR-P/XR-X/XR-M		●	●	●		●		
ROLLEI								
SL 2000 F/3003/3001	356 1)	●	●	●		●		
SL 66E/SL 66X/SL 66SE						●		
SL 6006/6002/6008		●		●		●		
2,8 GX						●		
YASHICA								
FX-DQuartz/107MP/108MP	380	●	●					
FX-3 Super/FX-7 Super		●						
FX-103		●	●	●		●		
230 AF		●	●	●		●		□
200 AF		●	●					□
270 AF		●	●					○
230 AF	381 AF	●	●	●		●		●
200 AF	381/2	●	●					●
270 AF	AF	●	●					○

● Function supported by adapter
□ Function not supported by adapter
○ Carried out by camera
1) Distributed by camera manufacturer
2) M1 and subsequent versions only
3) only with SCA 346/2 AF
4) only with SCA 373/2
6) M2 and subsequent versions only
7) M3 and subsequent versions only

Camera make and model	SCA adapter number	Ready light	Flash synch	Correct exposure light	Automatic aperture control	TTL flash control	Triggering control	Autofocus measuring beam

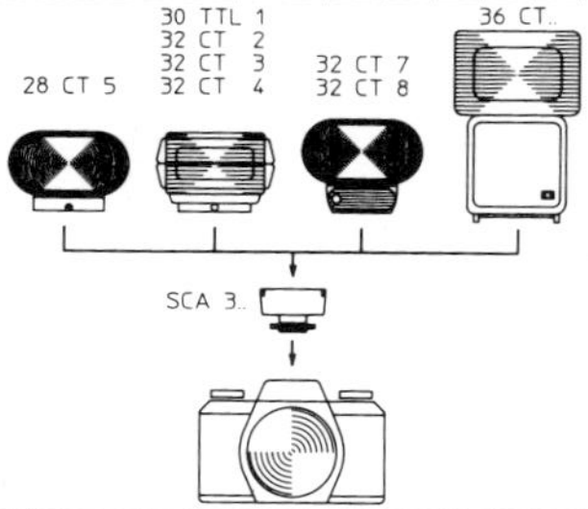

BRONICA

Camera make and model	SCA adapter number	Ready light	Flash synch	Correct exposure light	Automatic aperture control	TTL flash control	Triggering control	Autofocus measuring beam
mecablitz 28 CT..+G15, 30 TTL1+G15, 32 CT..+G15, 36 CT..+G15, 45 CT 3/4, 45 CL 3/4, 60 CT4 with ETRSi	386[1)]	●		●		●		
mecablitz 28 CT..+G15, 30 TTL1+G15, 32 CT..+G15, 36 CT..+G15, 45 CT 3/4, 45 CL 3/4, 60 CT4 with SQ-Ai	386[1)]	●		●		●		

CANON

Camera make and model	SCA adapter number	Ready light	Flash synch	Correct exposure light	Automatic aperture control	TTL flash control	Triggering control	Autofocus measuring beam
A-1/AE-1/F-1 New	310	●	●		●			
AE-1 Program		●	●	●	●			
AV-1/AL-1		●	●					
AT-1			●					
T 50/T 70/T 80		●	●		●			
T 90		●	●		●	□		
EOS 620/650		●	●			□		□
EOS 1/600/RT		●	●			□		□
EOS 10		●	●			□		○

MINOLTA

Camera make and model	SCA adapter number	Ready light	Flash synch	Correct exposure light	Automatic aperture control	TTL flash control	Triggering control	Autofocus measuring beam
X 300 S/X 370 N	331	●	●	●				
XD/XG/X 300/X 370		●	●	●				
X 700/X 500/X 570		●	●	●		●		
CLE		●	●	□		●	●	
5000/7000/9000		●	●	□		●		□
Maxxum 5000/7000/9000		●	●	□		○		□
Dynax/Maxxum/α	333/2 AF	●	●	●		●	●	●
3000 i/3700 i		●	●	●		●	●	●
5000 i[2)]/5700 i[2)]		●	●	●		●	●	●
7000 i/7700 i/8000 i		●	●	●		●	●	●
8700 i/7xi[6)]/3xi[2)]/SPxi/5xi/9xi[6)]........................		●	●	●		●	●	●

NIKON

Camera make and model	SCA adapter number	Ready light	Flash synch	Correct exposure light	Automatic aperture control	TTL flash control	Triggering control	Autofocus measuring beam
FE/EM/FG-20	343	●	●	●				
FM-2		●		●				
FE-2/FA/FG		●	●	●		●		
F 301/N 2000		●	●	●		●		
F 401/F 501/F 801/F 801s		●	●	●		●		□
N 4004/N 2020/N 8008		●	●	●		●		□
F 401s/ F 4/F4s		●	●	●		●		□
F 601M/N 6000		●	●	●		●		
F 601/N 6006/F 401x		●	●	□		●		□

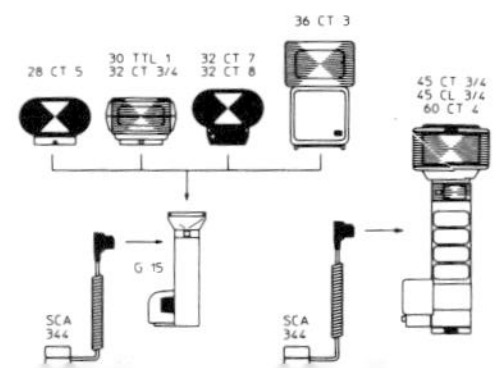

Camera make and model	SCA adapter number	Ready light	Flash synch	Correct exposure light	Automatic aperture control	TTL flash control	Triggering control	Autofocus measuring beam
OM-2 SP/OM -40		●	●	●		●	●	
OM-2						●	●	
OM-707/OM-77 AF		●	●	●		●	●	□
OM-101/OM-88		●	●	●		●	●	

Pentax

Camera make and model	SCA adapter number	Ready light	Flash synch	Correct exposure light	Automatic aperture control	TTL flash control	Triggering control	Autofocus measuring beam
LX (with finder shoe)	372	●	●	●		●	●	
ME-Super/ME-F/MG		●	●					
MV/MV-1		●	●	●				
Progr. A/A-3/A 3000		●	●	●	□			
Super A/645		●	●	●	□	●	●	
P 30/P 30 N/P 3 N		●	●	●	□			
P 30 T/P 50		●	●	●	□			
SFX/SF1		●	●	□		●	●	□
SFX$_N$/SF1$_N$/SF7/SF 10		●	●	□		●		□

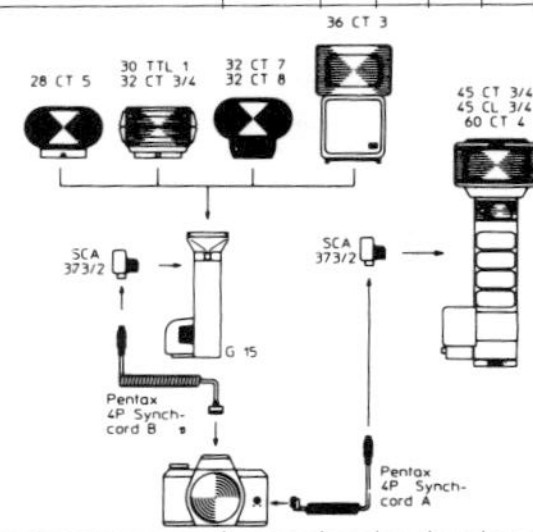

Camera make and model	SCA adapter number	Ready light	Flash synch	Correct exposure light	Automatic aperture control	TTL flash control	Triggering control	Autofocus measuring beam
mecablitz 28 CT..+G 15[4)], 30 TTL1+G 15[4)], 32 CT..+G 15[4)], 36 CT..+G 15[4)], 45 CT 3/4[4)], 45 CL 3/4[4)]	373 373/2 +							

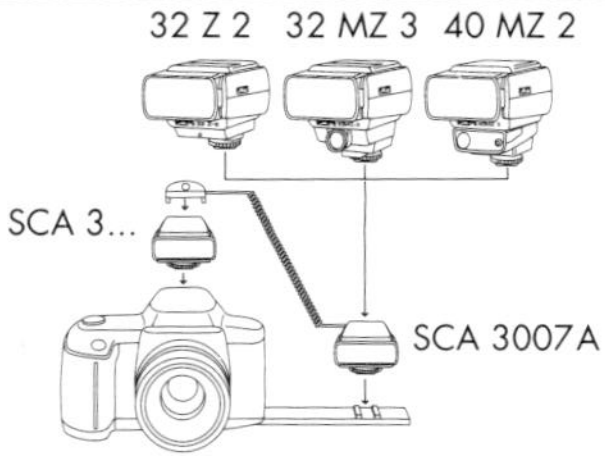

The connecting lead SCA 3007A permits the Metz mecablitz flashguns 32 Z 2, 32 MZ 3 and 40 MZ 2 to be separated from the camera whilst retaining the SCA 3000 functions.

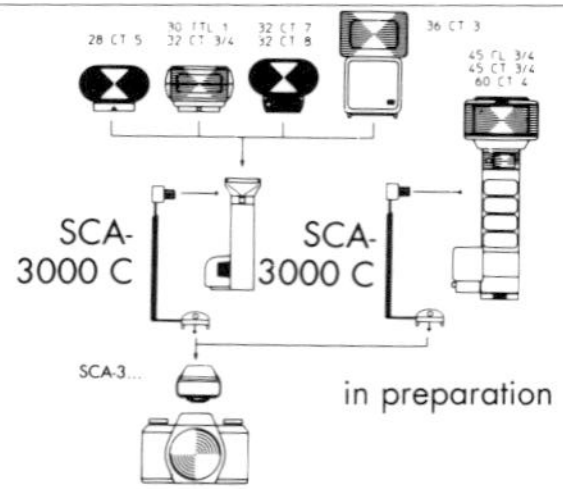

The connecting lead SCA 3000 C provides compatibility of SCA 3000 adapters with SCA 300 handle-mount flashguns and compact flashguns with power grip G 15.
Note: Not all SCA 3000 functions are supported.

3xi/5xi/7xi		●	●			●				●			●	●	
SPxi		●	●	●	●	●				●		●	●	●	●
9xi		●	●	●	●	●			●1)	●		●	●	●	●
si - series		●	●	●	●	●			●	●		●	●	●	●
NIKON AF	SCA-3401														
F 401/N 4004/F 401 S		●	●	●	●								●		●
F 401 X		●	●	●	●	●							●		●
F 501/N 2020		●	●	●	●								●		●
F 601 M/N 6000		●	●	●	●	●	●				●				●
F 601 AF/N 6006		●	●	●	●	●	●				●		●		●
F 801/F 8008/F 4/F 4 S		●	●	●	●	●	●				●	●	●	●	●
F 90/N 90		●	●	●	●	●	●				●	●	●	●	●
PENTAX AF	SCA-3701														
SFX/SF 1		●	●	●	●	●				●	●	●	●	●	●
SFX n/SF 1 n/SF 7/SF 10		●	●	●	●	●					●	●	●	●	●
Z1/Z 10/PZ 10		●	●	●	●	●					●	●	●	●	●
Z 20/PZ 20		●	●	●	●	●					●	●	●	●	●

* Flashgun permitting ● Provided
○ Fired by the camera 1) with Minolta control unit 2) with Minolta base FS 1200
□ Function not supported by adapter

SCA 3000 summary of functions

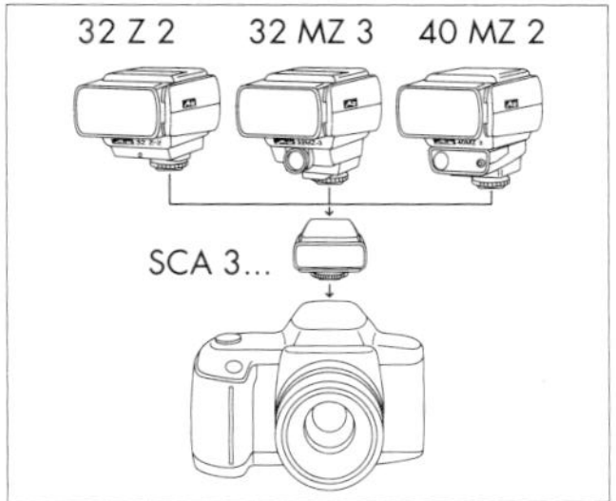

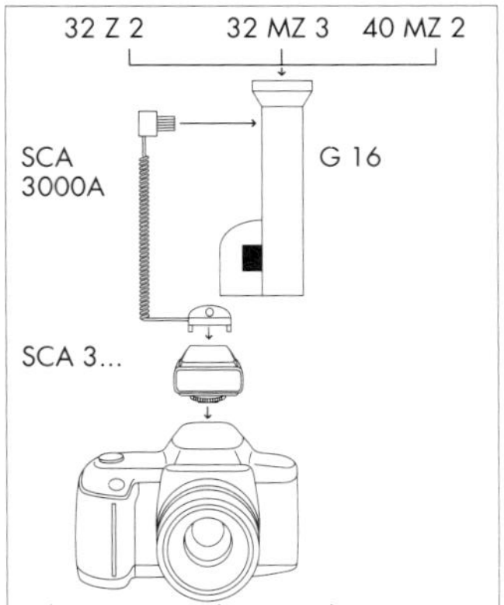

The connection between the Metz mecablitz flashguns 32 Z 2, 32 MZ 3 and 40 MZ 2 with power grip G 16 and an SCA 3000 adapter is

Camera	Adapter No.	Ready light in viewfinder	Correct exposure light in viewfinder	Auto flash synch	TTL flash control	TTL fill-in flash control	TTL flash exposure correction	A-TTL flash control	Cordless TTL flash control	Triggering control	Synchronization with 1st or 2nd shutter blind	Power zoom reflector control*	AF measuring beam control*	Display of flash range*	Automatic flash programmes
CANON	SCA-3101														
EOS 1/EOS 600		●		●	●	●	●	●			●	●	●	●	●
EOS 620/ EOS 630/ EOS 650/ EOS RT.................		●		●	●	●		●			●	●	●	●	●
EOS 10/EOS 10S...................		●		●	●	●		●			●	●	○	●	●
EOS 100/EOS ELAN...............		●		●	●	●	●	●			●	●	●	●	●
EOS 1000/EOS 1000F/ EOS 1000 FN/ EOS REBEL/EOS REBEL S........		●		●	●	●		●				●	●	●	●
EOS 700/EOS 750/EOS 850...				●	●	●		●				●	●	●	●
EOS 5/A2/E.........................		●		●	●	●	●	●			●	●	○	●	●
MINOLTA	SCA-3301														
5000[2]/7000[2]/9000[2]		●	●	●	●							●	□	●	●
Dynax/Maxxum/α:															
[illegible]		●	●	●	●					●		●	●	●	●

The SCA 300 and 3000 Systems	
300 A Adapter cable for handle-mount flash and Power grip G 15	
3000 A Adapter cable for handle-mount flash and Power grip G 15	
301 Standard foot	
310, 311, 312 AF, 312/2 AF-	Canon
3101	Canon-EOS and A2/A2E
320, 321	Olympus, Praktica
330, 331, 332, 333/2 AF	Minolta
3301	Minolta Maxxum/Dynax i, xi, si
340, 341, 342, 343, 344, 345, 346 AF, 346/2 AF	Nikon
3401	Nikon AF-Cameras
350, 351	Leica
356	Rollei
360	Cosina
363, 364	Ricoh
366	Chinon
370,371, 372, 373, 373/2, 374/2 AF	Pentax
3701	Pentax AF-Cameras
380	Contax, Yashica
381 AF, 381/2 AF	Yashica
386	Bronica
390	Hasselblad

Use with older Metz flash units: The SCA 500C converter is used to adapt older Mecablitz 45 CT 5 and 60 CT 2 flash units to the more universal SCA 300 system. This converter connects both systems.

Digital Control with the SCA 3000 System

While the SCA 500 and 300 adapter systems use analog control technology, the expanded SCA 3000 system introduced at Photokina '92 uses digital control signals. This system, developed as an improvement of the successful SCA 300 system, can analyze and evaluate a camera's control system and transfer information digitally. With the SCA 3000 adapter system, the film speed and aperture value are transferred digitally from the camera to the flash unit (with compatible camera systems). Also, matrix and multiple-field exposure measurements may be utilized for TTL flash measurement, with cameras that provide these functions. The new adapter also provides functions such as automatic control of the flash unit's zoom head setting, and wireless TTL flash control. With the SCA 3000 system, even Nikon's "D" technology autofocus (AF) flash can be integrated in the flash unit.

Use with SCA 300 adapters: It is important to note that all SCA 3000 flash units can also be used with SCA 300 system adapters. However, not all SCA 3000 system functions will be supported. In addition, handle-mount flash units of the 300 system (the Metz Mecablitz 45 CL 3 and 45 CL 4), and compact SCA 300 flash units used with the Power Grip G 15, become autofocus compatible by using the SCA 3000 C red light cable and the appropriate 3000 system adapter.

Advantages of the SCA 3000 system: The SCA 3000 adapter system offers any photographer considerable advantages. It increases the choice of flash units that are compatible with nearly any camera. Also, the system allows using special flash techniques, such as wireless TTL flash mode, with cameras that provide TTL metering. (Until now this has been possible only with Minolta xi, si cameras and the associated Minolta flash units.)

There are also the advantages of an integrated auxiliary flash unit, a stroboscopic flash feature, and manual selection of light output for all operating modes, with the exception of fully automatic programmed mode. The only option not available with SCA adapters at the time this book was printed is "stroboscopic continuous light" permitting super-high flash (FP) synchronization speeds of up to 1/4000 second with the Nikon N90/F90 camera and Nikon SB-25 flash unit.

The advantages of the SCA adapter system are obvious. If a camera of a different brand is used, only a new adapter is needed. If cameras of the same brand with additional features are introduced, only a new adapter is required. Therefore, a single flash unit can be used with the most diverse adapters and camera systems. This can be important for a professional photographer who uses several camera systems, and for amateur photographers when two or three different camera systems are used within a family, in a club, or among a group of friends.

SCA Adapter System Control Options

This overview illustrates all the adapter-controlled technical options offered by SCA adapters, provided these options are offered by the camera system. Some of these functions can be performed either individually or in combination.

Automatic flash sync speed setting: In many modern reflex cameras the camera is automatically set to the fastest sync speed when the flash unit has recycled to 70% of full output power. (Some camera models set a slower default speed.) When the flash-ready indicator goes out after a flash has been fired or when the unit has been switched off, usually the original shutter speed is reset.

Flash-ready indication: All metering flash operations are displayed on the flash unit and, depending on the camera type, are also displayed in the camera's viewfinder. The flash unit will fire only when the flash-ready indicator lamp is lit. As a precaution, after it is lit, allow a few moments to pass before firing. If a flash is fired too soon, underexposure may occur because most cameras indicate flash readiness after the flash recycles to a charge of 70%. This 70% readiness is not important with TTL flash metering in the close-up or normal distance range because this output is usually adequate for a correct flash exposure.

Correct exposure indication: After the flash has been fired the camera signals that the flash exposure was technically correct or that there is a risk of an exposure error. (The signal is different from system to system.) This signal is generated in TTL and automatic flash modes. If the camera does not have an appropriate display, simply look at the back of the flash unit to see whether the exposure was correct. An LED will light up to indicate correct exposure.

TTL flash control: More than 250 SLR cameras are compatible with the SCA system and allow measuring and controlling the flash from Metz Mecablitz units.

Various SCA system-controlled flash techniques will be discussed later. The following flash control options require the 300 or 3000 system:

- TTL fill flash control
- A-TTL flash control
- Programmed automatic flash

Wireless TTL flash control with SCA 3000: Wireless TTL flash control is also known as "TTL remote operation." In wireless remote flash control, the flash unit mounted to the camera controls additional flash units thereby extending automatic exposure metering and control to all flash units. For remote flash control of multiple Metz Mecablitz 40 MZ 2 flash units the auxiliary flash units require a SCA 3080 slave adapter. (See box for further information on using wireless multiple flash.)

Triggering control: This feature prevents a flash from firing if it would result in overexposure due to ambient light. This is particularly important with older equipment, because flash exposure programs could not be set for fill flash and in these situations the apertures would not close automatically.

TTL flash exposure correction: A flash exposure correction affects exposure by changing the amount of light output by the flash rather than the aperture or shutter speed. The total exposure value — whether adjusted toward the plus or minus range or not at all — remains. This technical feature is offered by only a few cameras, including all Nikon and Canon AF models.

Second curtain sync: Firing the flash as the exposure is ending, just before the second shutter curtain covers the film again, instead at the beginning of the exposure is called second curtain or rear curtain sync. Using fill flash with second curtain sync causes the blur of moving objects, caused by the ambient light, to trail behind the objects instead of appearing in front of them, making a more natural-looking picture. Second curtain sync can be set with the SCA 3000 adapters, provided it is a feature offered by the camera.

Power zoom reflector control: Metz Mecablitz flash units with the "MZ" designation allow a camera's microprocessor to automatically set the flash's zoom reflector to the match the focal length of the lens. This ensures the flash unit's angle of illumination will match the lens' angle of coverage. Power zooms can also be set manually, if the camera does not offer this feature.

Autofocus illuminator or pre-flash: The SCA 300 system includes a red light adapter for this special function of certain AF cameras. A pre-flash function is already integrated in basic SCA 3000 system units. The pre-flash is activated by the camera under conditions of low ambient light, low subject contrast or other conditions that interfere with AF sensor operation. The pre-flashes project a light pattern on the subject which the camera utilizes for automatic focusing.

Shooting distance range display: With the SCA 3000 Metz flash units, it is possible to display the shooting distance range on the LCD, provided the camera has the appropriate features.

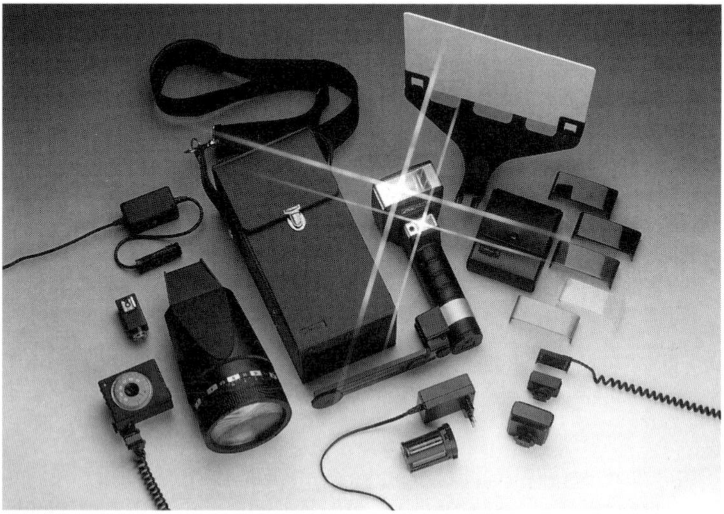

An illustration of the many accessories available for the Metz 45 series flash units.

Automatic aperture control: The aperture set on the flash unit will automatically set the aperture on the camera lens.

SCA 300 and 3000 System Accessories

Power grip G 15: This accessory converts SCA 300 shoe-mount flash units into handle-mount units for easier handling. Since it accepts C size alkaline or NiCd batteries, it increases the number of flashes and is recommended for longer shoots.

Power grip G 16: This accessory is similar to the Power grip G 15 except it is designed to be used with SCA 3000 shoe-mount flash units.

SCA 3000 A red light system adapter: This coiled cord connects all SCA 3000 modules to the Power grip G 16. It features a built-in autofocus measuring sensor for accuracy of focus when the flash is off-camera.

SCA 3000 C red light system converter: This coiled cord adds a built-in autofocus illuminator to SCA 300 system handle-mount flash units or the Power grip G 15 when used with the appropriate camera and SCA 3000 adapter.

SCA 3007 A red light coiled cord: This 4-1/2 foot extension cord allows the use of System 3000 compact flash units off-camera while maintaining all dedicated functions. The end of the cable that connects to the camera has an autofocus illumination unit to aid cameras with autofocus.

SCA 3080 slave adapter: This special accessory for wireless TTL flash control can currently be used only with the 40 MZ 2 unit. Every 40 MZ 2 unit used remotely requires an SCA 3080 slave adaptor.

SCA 305 A TTL multiconnector: Up to three SCA flash units can be automatically controlled by the camera in TTL flash metering mode. Up to seven flash units may be controlled by stacking TTL multiconnectors.

SCA 305 K cord: Connects shoe-mount flash units with the TTL multiconnector for multiple flash use.

SCA 305 S cord: Connects handle-mount units with the TTL multiconnector for multiple flash use.

SCA 305 V5 cord: This cord can be added to either the 305 K or 305 S cords above to extend their length by 16 feet.

SCA 500 C converter: This is used to adapt older Metz Mecablitz 45 CT 5 and 60 CT 2 flash units to the more universal SCA 300 system. This converter connects both systems.

Which SCA Adapter for Which System?

Each SCA adapter is identified by a number, for example, 301, 351 or 3301. The SCA 300 system identifies each major SLR camera system in number groups of 10 while the SCA 3000 system uses groups of 100.

The digital sequence from 300 to 310 and from 3000 to 3100 is used exclusively for adapters and general Metz flash accessories. For example, SCA 301 is the identification number for the standard adapter for hot shoe and cable contacts via the synchronization terminal.

Identification by number group: SCA adapters for Canon cameras are always identified by the first group of 10. For example, the 310 adapter is the first one built for Canon cameras, SCA 312/2 is the second version of the Canon adapter (for the EOS system) and, as opposed to the SCA 311, can also control autofocus monitor pre-flashes.

In an analogous fashion, the first 100 numbers of the 3000 System are used exclusively for Canon cameras, for example, the SCA 3101 is the adapter ID for the EOS-system. For specific information refer to the charts on pages 38-41.

Compatibility with earlier systems: All earlier adapter versions are compatible within the 300 system. A photographer who has an earlier SCA adapter flash unit and changes his camera system, requiring another adapter, may conveniently connect his latest adapter version without problems. However, the available functions can only be those for which the flash unit is designed and which can be controlled by the camera and flash unit combination.

Lack of standardization: This multitude of adapters is required because of a lack of standardization among the camera manufacturers. For example, Nikon takes a simple approach by integrating only the flash metering sensor in the camera housing and putting the entire electronic control assembly in the flash unit. Olympus and Minolta have mostly or completely integrated the electronic control components in the camera housing, and the flash unit only receives information concerning the flash output.

Actually only three contact points are required to transfer information between the camera and flash: for firing, TTL metering and automatic flash aperture control. Thanks to the SCA 300 and 3000 systems, the photographer need not worry about the compatibility of flash and camera.

How to use the SCA system: To use SCA adaptors, all the photographer needs to know is which adapter is required for their camera system and which accessories would be beneficial to them. For camera-specific information about the various adapters, refer to the charts on pages 38-41.

For cameras without hot shoes or flash dedication systems: For cameras without a hot shoe contact — older models and most medium and large format cameras — a synchronization cable can be used between the SCA 301 standard foot and the camera's PC sync terminal.

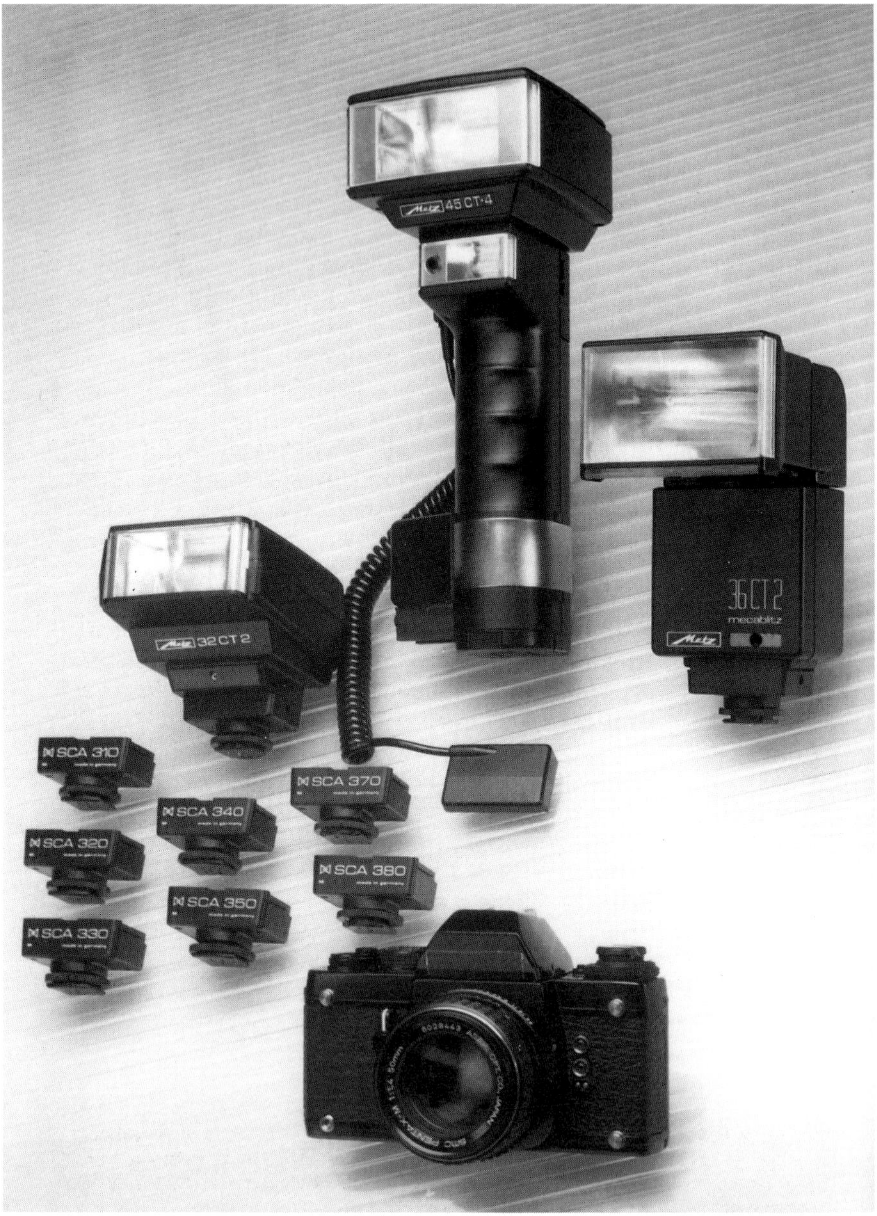
45 CT-4
32 CT 2
36CT 2
mecablitz
SCA 310
SCA 320
SCA 330
SCA 340
SCA 350
SCA 370
SCA 380

The Metz Mecablitz Product Line

Metz Mecablitz Flash Units

Metz manufactures a wide range of flash units for both amateur and professional use. Many of the small flash units are not available in the United States but are found in other markets such as Canada. There are only a few Metz flash units that are not included in the SCA 300 or SCA 3000 System.

The first number in every Metz model number indicates the power output; it is the metric guide number for ISO 100 film. (For readers used to thinking in feet rather than meters, multiplying a metric guide number by 3.3 converts it into a "foot" guide number). Thus the Metz 40 MZ 2, with a full-power metric guide number of 40, has a full-power guide number of 132 when expressed in feet, that is, an aperture of f/11 at twelve feet. This means a unit with the metric guide number 28 in its model designation outputs twice as much light as a unit with a 20 in its designation. *Guide numbers are covered in detail in Chapter 1.*

In addition to the guide number, the product identification includes letters that provide further information about the unit's characteristics. The letter C indicates the flash unit has at least one photocell, or telecomputer, as Metz calls it, to meter the light output for automatic flash control. MZ in the name refers to a motorized zoom reflector, while Z alone indicates a manually adjusted zoom reflector.

If the sequence of characters ends with a digit, the number 1 as in 45 CL 1 or 60 CT 1, denotes a basic flash unit, with basic features. A higher number at the end, as in 45 CL 3 or CL 4, indicates a more luxurious model that offers greater features and ease

⇦ **Metz has a wide variety of flash models to meet every photographers' needs. Mecablitz 32 CT 2, 36 CT 2 and 45 CT 4 units are shown here with some of the special SCA adapters that allow them to take advantage of the SCA 300-specific features.**

of operation. For example, the Mecablitz 45 CL 4 includes a secondary reflector and LED indicators.

The two features common to all Metz Mecablitz flash units are a "flash ready" indicator and manual flash control. It can be assumed every Metz flash unit is equipped with these functions, although they are not mentioned in every flash description.

Compact Flash Units

Mecablitz 20 B 5 and 20 BC 6

These are the smallest flash units in the Metz Mecablitz product line, sized to fit in any camera bag (width 3″ x height 2.1″ x depth 3.4″). As indicated by the model number, the flash units have a metric guide number of 20. Both units accept only standard AA alkaline batteries and come with a clip-on wide angle diffuser. Neither unit has a tilting flash head.

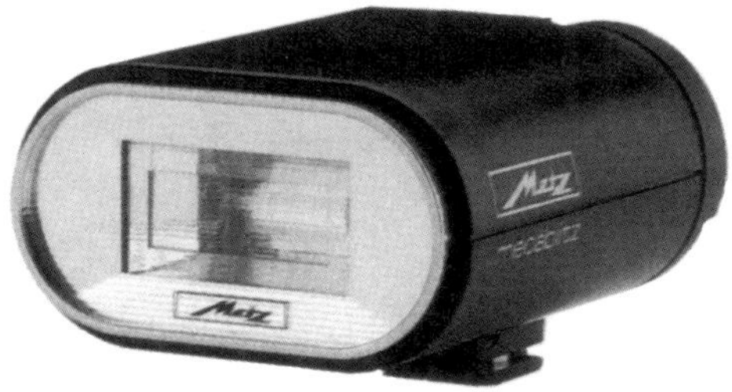

The Metz Mecablitz 20 B 5 is a compact, manual flash unit. It has a control dial to calculate the aperture value for a given subject distance.

The Mecablitz 20 B 5 provides manual flash mode only, so the user must calculate the required f/stop. The 20 BC 6 features a photocell that controls flash output. The 20 BC 6 permits using only one f/stop in automatic mode. The specific aperture depends

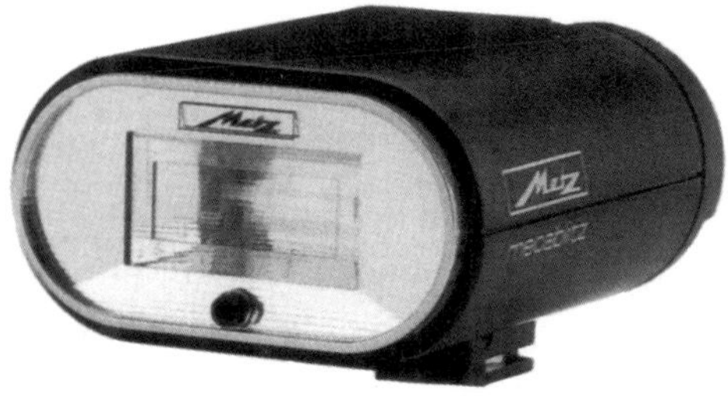

The small round dot beneath the flash head of the Metz Mecablitz 20 BC 6 is the photocell or sensor which regulates the flash duration for correct exposure.

on the speed of the film being used. Color codes on the back of the flash unit indicate the correct aperture and the flash range in automatic mode.

Mecablitz 30 B 3i and 30 BCT 4i

The Mecablitz 30 B 3i features only manual flash control. It has a battery test indicator and automatic unit shut-off. Energy-saving circuitry extends the life of a fresh set of alkaline batteries to approximately 150 flash exposures. Both units can use alkaline batteries or environmentally-sound, rechargeable NiCd batteries.

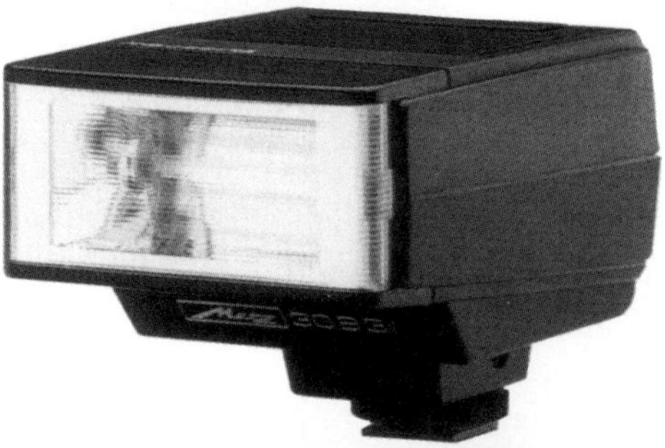

Metz 30 B 3i and 30 BCT 4i units feature a tilting flash head to bounce the light.

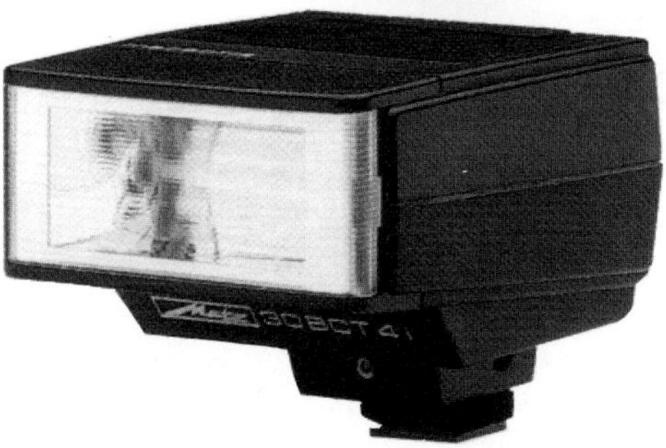

The photocell or sensor in the Metz Mecablitz 30 BCT 4i automatically regulates the flash duration for correct exposure. This unit is designed for cameras that have only a single hot-shoe contact and thus, no camera/flash dedication.

The Mecablitz 30 BCT 4i is more luxurious though it is still not part of the SCA system. In addition to the features of the 30 B 3i, the 30 BCT 4i offers a photocell which regulates light output, and its thyristor circuit assures low power consumption. The unit allows the photographer to choose from three automatic apertures, and a "Flash-OK" signal confirms correct flash exposure. Flash capacity is a maximum 1,500 flashes per charge with NiCd batteries or 3,500 with alkaline batteries.

For indirect (bounce) lighting, both units have tilting flash heads. Each unit is supplied with a clip-on wide angle diffuser.

Mecablitz 30 TTL 1i, 30 TTL 1i AF and 32 CT 3i

The 30 TTL 1i and 30 TTL 1i AF are identical flash units. However, the latter is supplied as a kit with the appropriate SCA 300 AF adapter for a Canon, Minolta or Nikon autofocus camera. It provides AF illumination to assist the camera's autofocus system in difficult lighting or contrast conditions.

The 30 TTL 1i is one of Metz' high power compact flash units. It allows flash exposure control using the camera's TTL metering system.

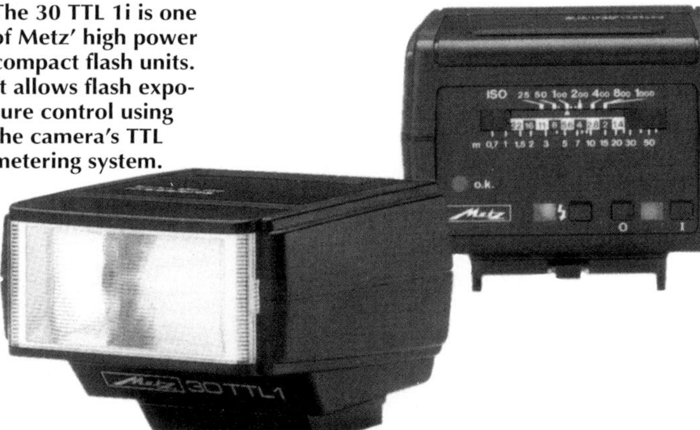

The 30 TTL 1i AF is simply the 30 TTL 1i flash unit coupled with an SCA 300 AF adaptor for a Canon EOS, Nikon AF or Minolta Maxxum/ Dynax camera.

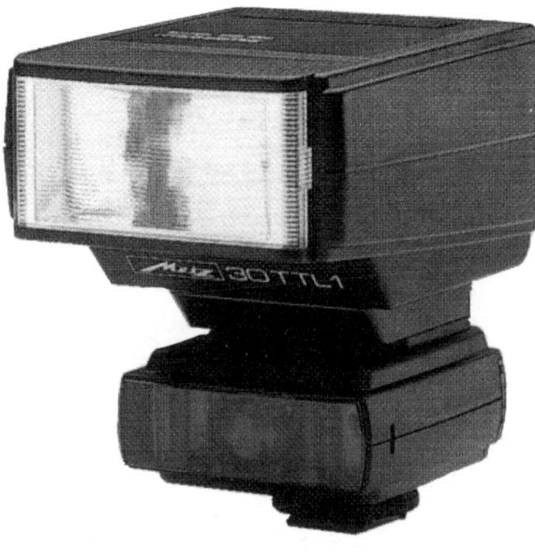

The 30 TTL 1i and 32 CT 3i share many of the same features. Both are full-fledged members of the SCA family and provide TTL flash control with cameras that feature TTL metering. The units feature 90 degrees vertical tilt and 180 degrees horizontal rotation, a "Flash-OK" indicator, a battery tester, and automatic unit shut-off. Alkaline or rechargeable NiCd batteries may be used. Flash capacity is a maximum 1,500 flashes per charge with NiCd batteries or 3,500 with alkaline batteries. The units are equipped with the more advanced IGBT light output control described in Chapter 1. Each is supplied with a clip-on wide angle diffuser. Both can be set manually.

The obvious difference between the two models is the slightly higher guide number of the 32 CT 3i. In addition, the 30 TTL 1i has no photocell and therefore, no automatic flash mode. The 32 CT 3i does have automatic flash control which allows the photographer three working apertures.

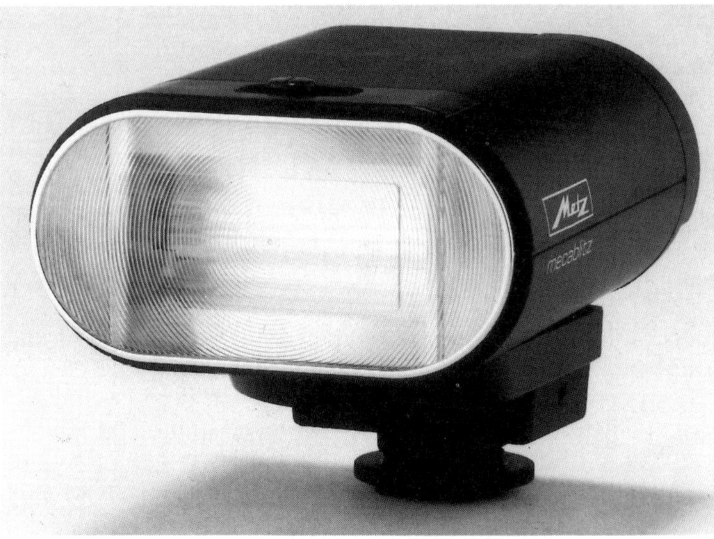

The Metz Mecablitz 28 CT 5 is a versatile compact flash unit which is compatible with the SCA 300 Adapter System. It features a guide number of 28, a three-position manual zoom flash head, 90 degree tilt, and thyristor-controlled automatic exposure.

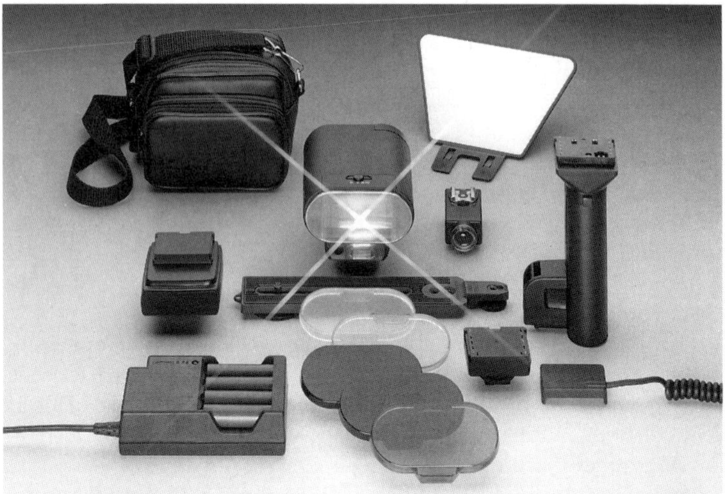

Available accessories for Metz flash units, such as this Mecablitz 32 CT 7, include a bounce diffusers and a color filter set.

Mecablitz 28 CT 5 and 32 CT 7

There are relatively minor differences between the Mecablitz 28 CT 5 and the 32 CT 7. The 32 CT 7 has a higher guide number and is noticeably taller. The height is due to a secondary flash head under the main reflector, which, in bounce flash mode, provides approximately 10 to 15% of forward fill. Although both units have automatic shut-off, only the 32 CT 7 has manual override.

Both units offer winder mode with 2 exposures per sec, which reduces the flash output to a metric guide number of 5 at ISO 100. The manual zoom function has settings for 28, 35 and 50-250 mm coverage. The flash heads have a 102 degree vertical tilt range which includes 12 degrees downward tilt to prevent the problem of insufficient illumination in the lower part of a close-up picture. The horizontal rotation range is 270 degrees to allow more bounce lighting options.

These compact models are SCA compatible. Both offer TTL mode, as well as, thyristor-controlled, automatic flash exposure with three working apertures. Additional features include "Flash-OK" indicator, battery tester and an easily visible LED indicator.

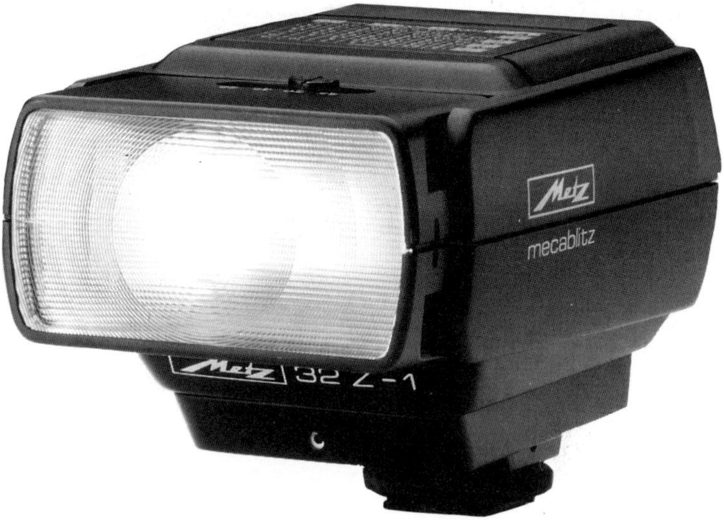

The Metz Mecablitz 32 Z 1 has not been integrated in the SCA 3000 System thus, it features telecomputer mode only. The "Z" in the model designation indicates that the flash head zooms to match the coverage of lens focal lengths of 28, 35, 50 and 85mm.

Mecablitz 32 Z 1, 32 Z 2 and 32 MZ 3

These three flash units offer the same guide number and basic functions, and are quite user-friendly. All three feature LED indicators, winder mode allowing two exposures per second, "Flash OK" indicator, a battery tester, automatic unit shut-off, and an IGBT control of light quantity. Lithium, alkaline, or rechargeable NiCd batteries can be used with all three units.

Metz has managed to keep this series quite compact, measuring 3 inches wide, approximately 3.5 inches high (depending on the adapter used), and 5 inches deep (2.8 cm x 8 to 9 cm x 12 cm). However, their weight of about 11 ounces (300 grams) each means these units are not extreme lightweights. The flash heads of all three units can be tilted to an angle of 13 degrees below horizontal for close-ups, and upward, up to 90 degrees, for bounce flash. The horizontal rotation range is 270 degrees.

All three units have a built-in telecomputer with 3 working apertures, and the resultant shooting ranges are displayed clearly

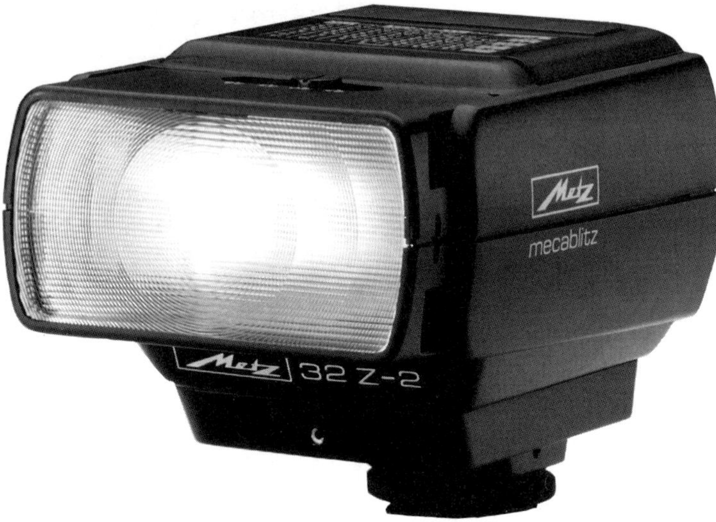

The Metz Mecablitz 32 Z 2 has been integrated fully in the SCA 3000 Adapter System and features a "Flash OK" confirmation signal, battery tester, automatic shut-off and state-of-the-art IGBT light output control.

on the aperture computer on the back of the flash unit. Of course, film speed and guide number variations due to different reflector settings will be adjusted automatically.

The 32 Z 1 is the most basic in the series. It is one of the few flash units in the entire Metz line that is not integrated into the SCA adapter system. Both the 32 Z 2 and 32 MZ 3 are compatible with SCA 300 and 3000 adaptors. In addition, both flash units offer TTL flash control, provided it is a camera feature and the appropriate SCA adaptor is used.

The designation "MZ" indicates the 32 MZ 3 has a motorized zoom head with settings for 28, 35, 50 and 85mm lenses. The flash unit's motor drive sets the flash head based on focal length information received from the camera. The units with only a "Z" in the model description have a manually adjustable zoom head with the same four settings. The other advanced feature of the Mecablitz 32 MZ 3 is an integral, autofocus assist beam, effective with autofocus cameras up to a distance of approximately 30 feet (9 m) in total darkness.

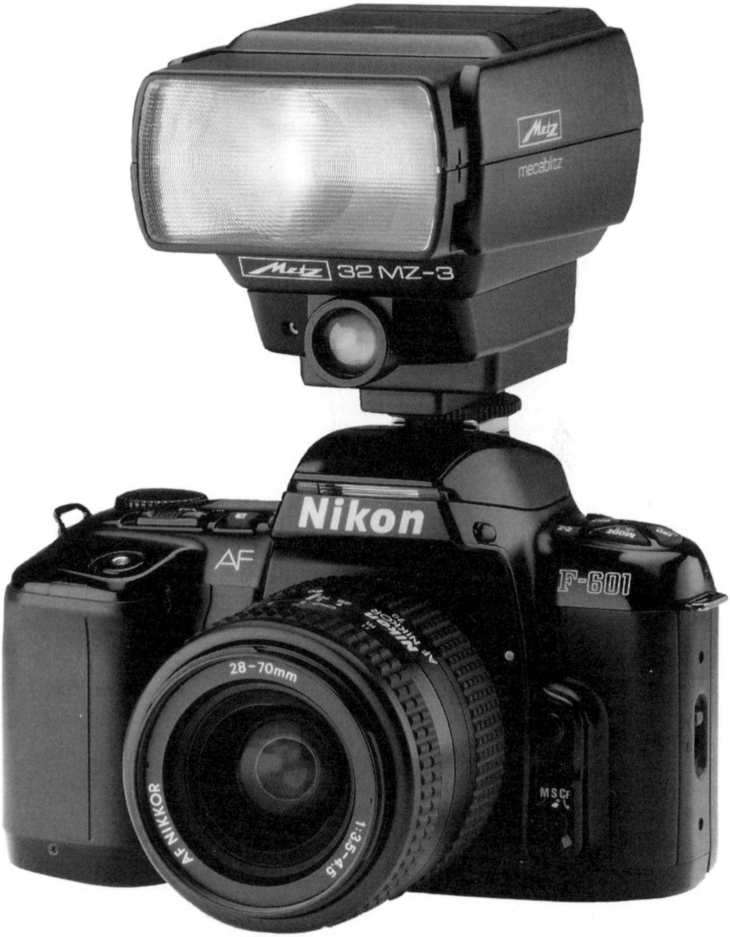

The Metz Mecablitz 32 MZ 3 includes a red light autofocus illuminator, centered just below the flash head. Its purpose is to assist AF cameras in dark or low contrast situations.

I

Pictures a and b: Since it is not always possible to chose the time of day for taking a picture, flash is an important tool for eliminating color shifts and highlighting detail. In this case, using fill-flash added definition and color to these photos of Moroccan street vendors.

Pictures c and d: Picture d was taken with a Canon EOS Elan using fill-flash in fully automatic program mode. In standard "P" Program mode (picture c) the photographer had to decide whether or not to use flash.

Pictures e and f: If high-speed film (ISO 400 or faster) is used, illumination of large interiors or even an entire cupola, such as that of the Blue Mosque in Istanbul, can be successfully accomplished with flash. Even pictures such as these which illustrate natural colors and richness of detail may be taken without complex exposure calculations.

II

Picture a: The catchlights in the model's eyes reveal that fill-flash was used to reduce the deep shadows on the face, creating a less contrasty, more pleasing photograph. The EOS Elan's microprocessor automatically controlled the duration of the flash.

Pictures b and c: Should conditions require that pictures be taken in the direct, unflattering light of high noon, the proper use of fill-flash will reduce shadows under the model's eyes and on her neck. If, as in this case, automatic TTL fill flash mode is not a dedicated camera option, the photographer should pre-select an aperture which is 1-1/2 to 2 f/stops greater than the one in use on the lens while using the flash in A mode.

III

Pictures a and b: An entire building may be illuminated with flash, if a high-speed film such as Agfachrome 1000 (in this case) is used. In the top picture (a) flash was used to balance the ambient light exposure. In the bottom picture (b), the fastest possible flash sync speed was automatically selected by the camera during the TTL flash exposure, producing an entirely different effect.

IV

A different color rendition is achieved by using flash. The warm tone of the existing light in picture a was eliminated by the use of flash in picture b.

Pictures c and d: The extreme contrast of the scene (d) was beyond the exposure latitude of the transparency film being used. By using fill flash (c), the contrast was reduced, changing the overall character and color rendition of the finished result.

Pictures e and f: In this case fill flash was used to increase contrast and separate the subject from the background. The short flash duration also assured a sharp image by eliminating the possibility of camera shake from the otherwise slow, handheld exposure (f).

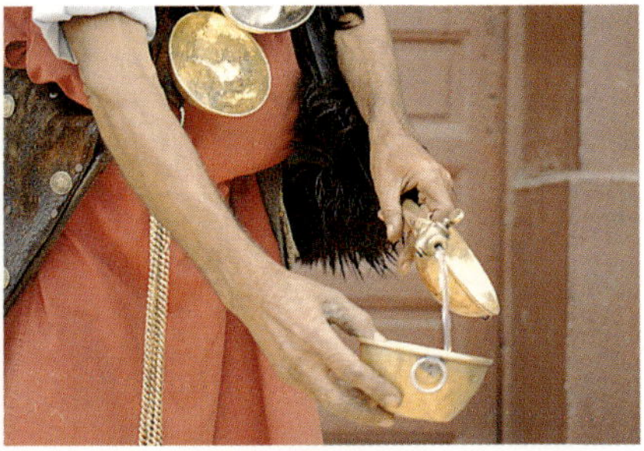

a

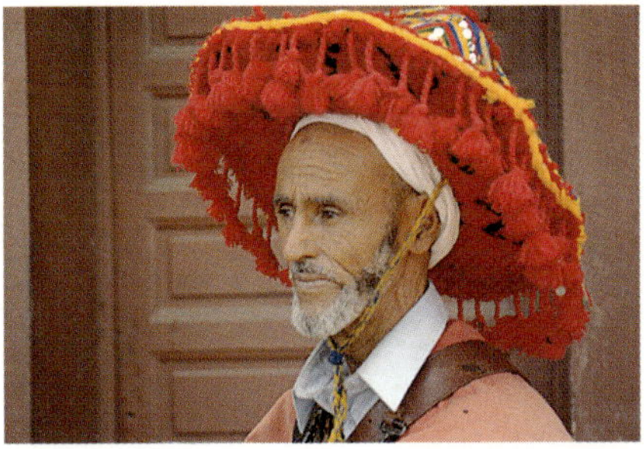

b

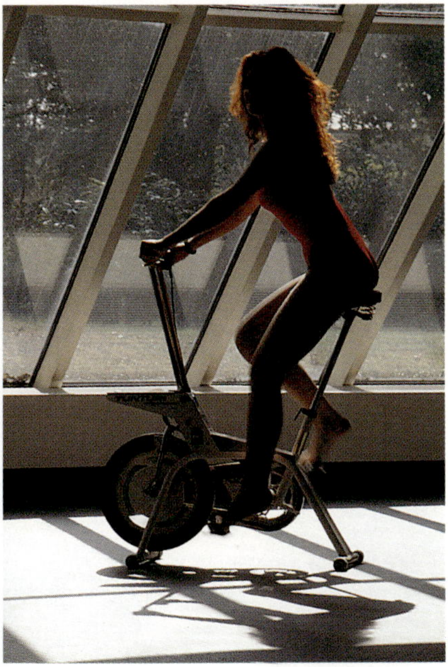

c

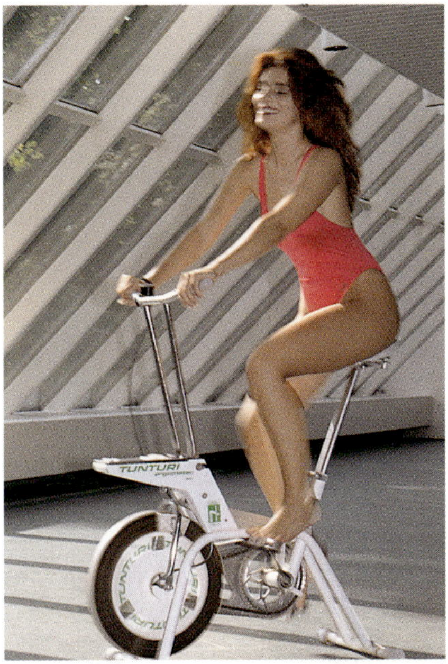

d

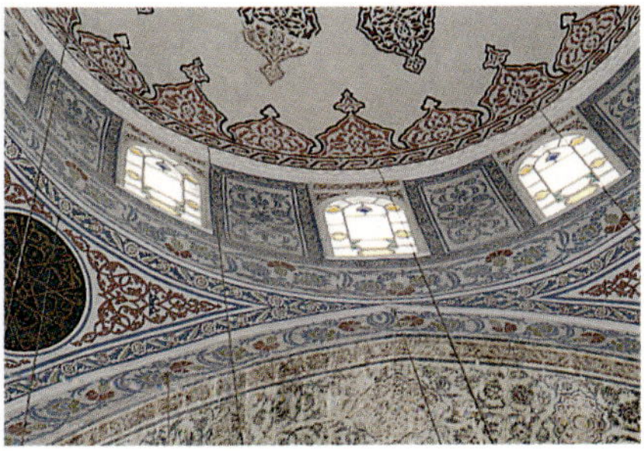

e

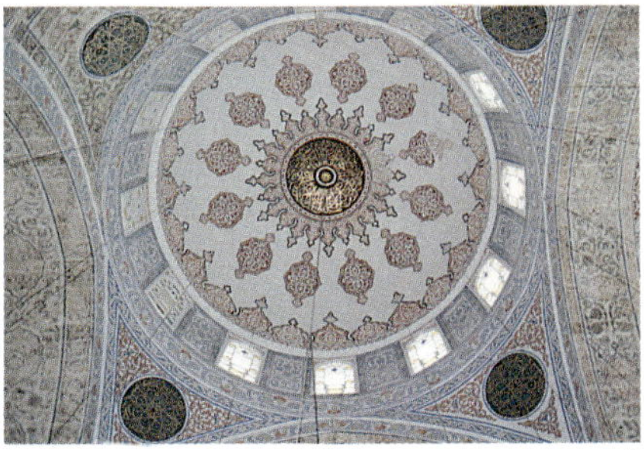

f

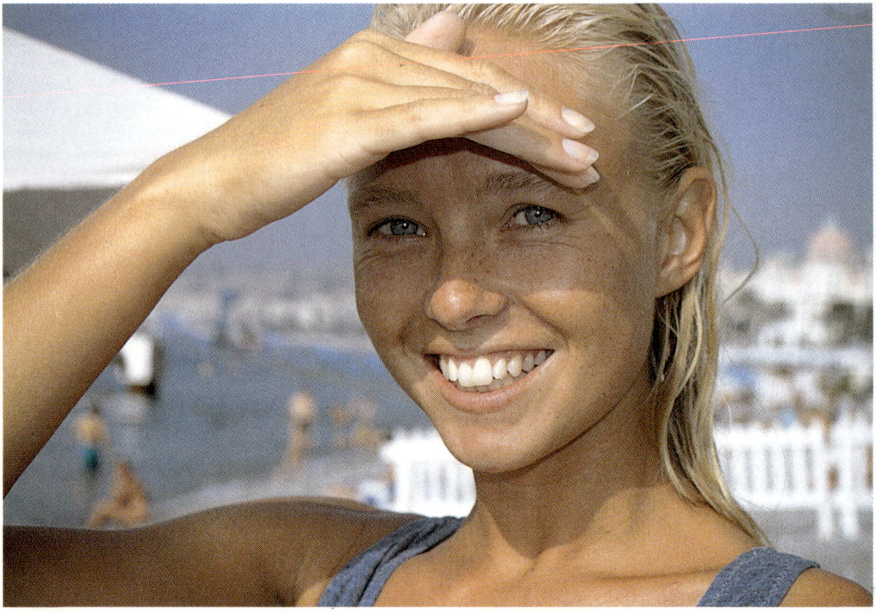

a

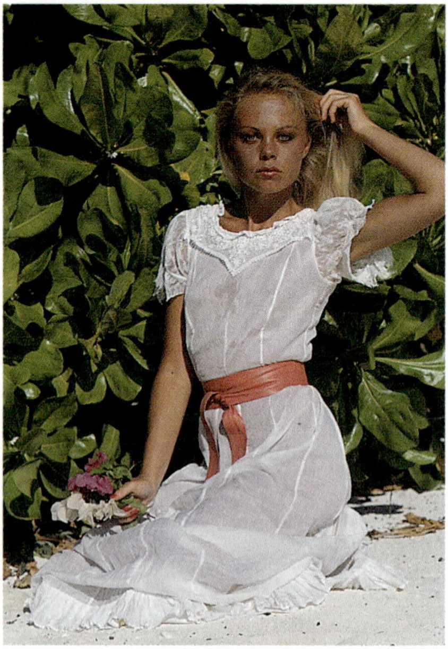

b

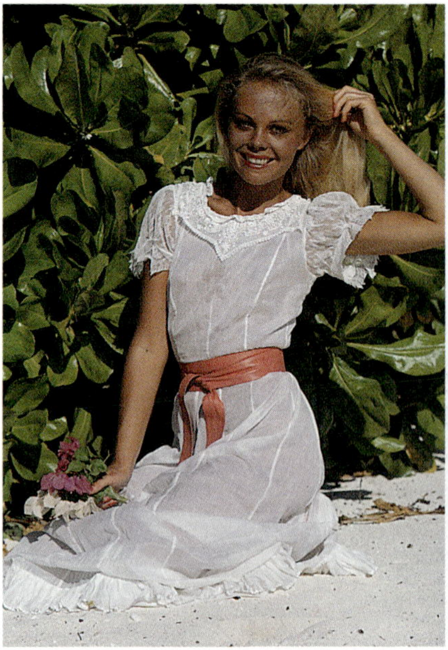

c

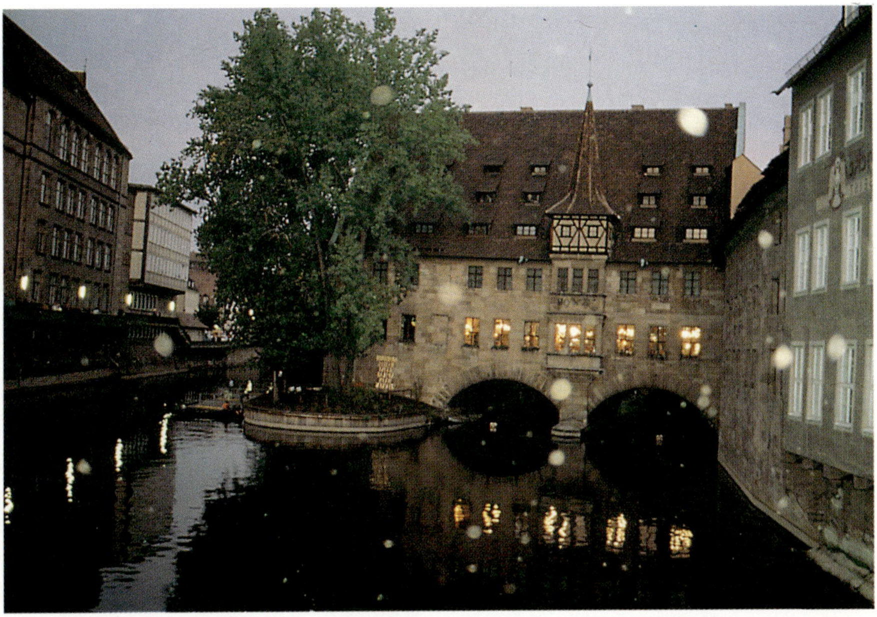

a

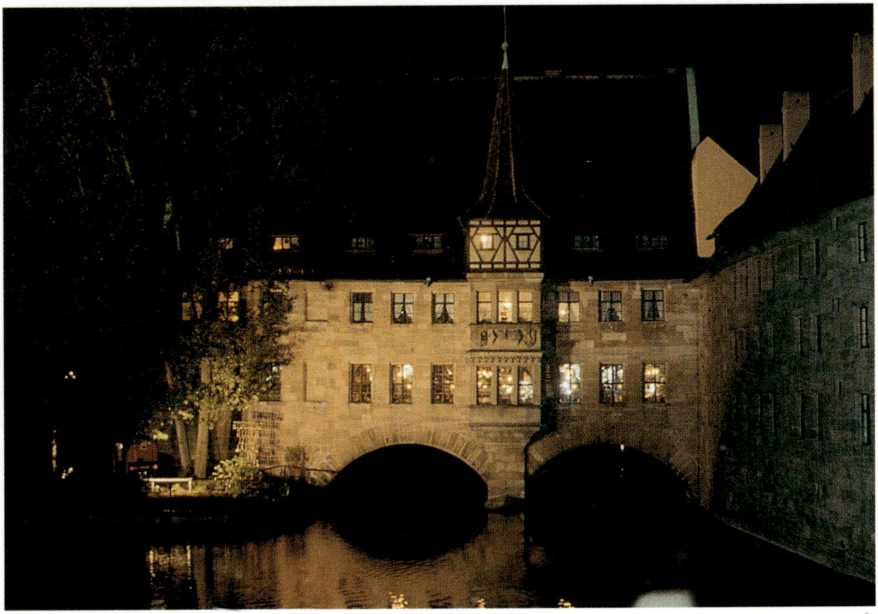

b

– Tafel III –

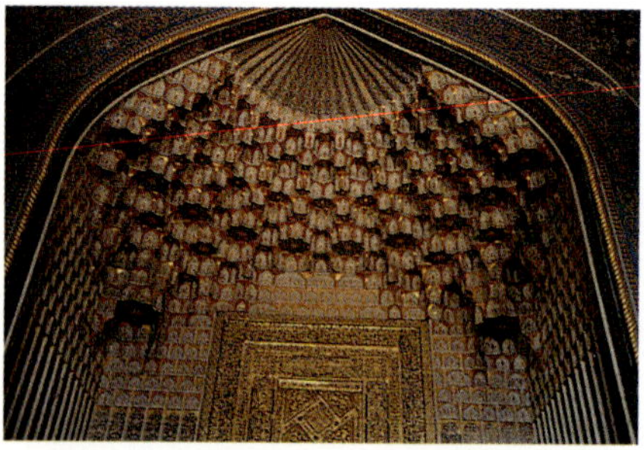

a

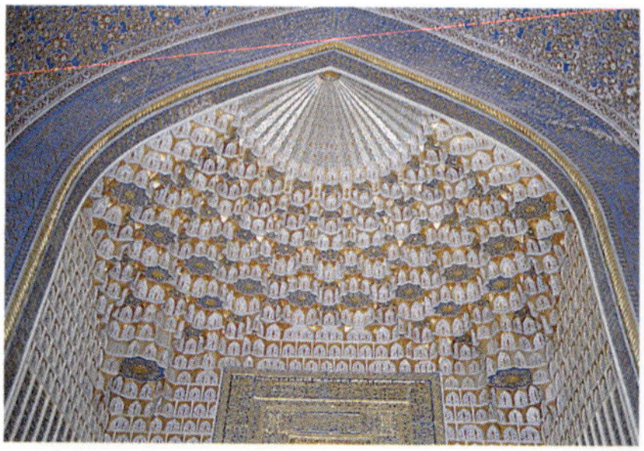

b

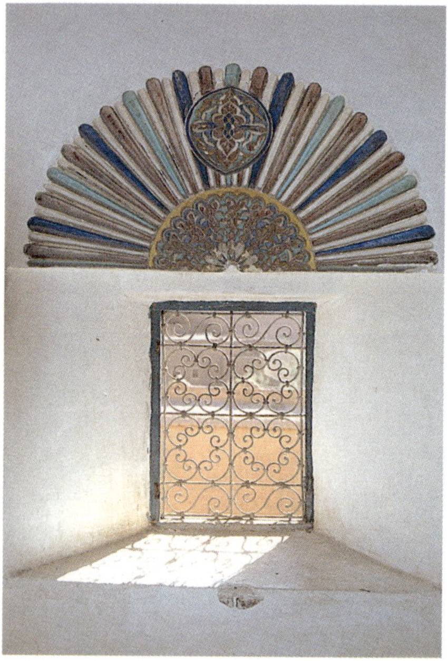

c

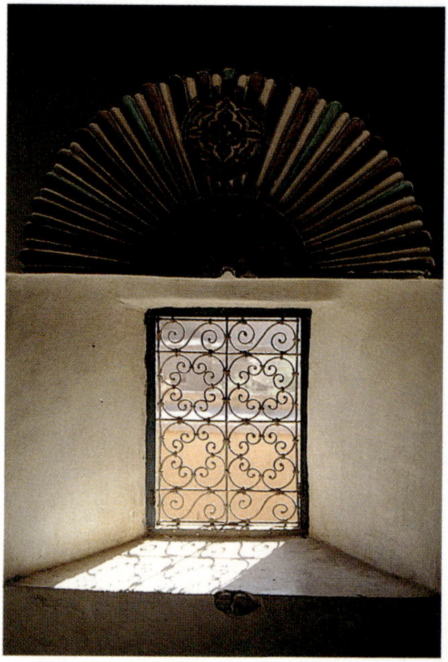

d

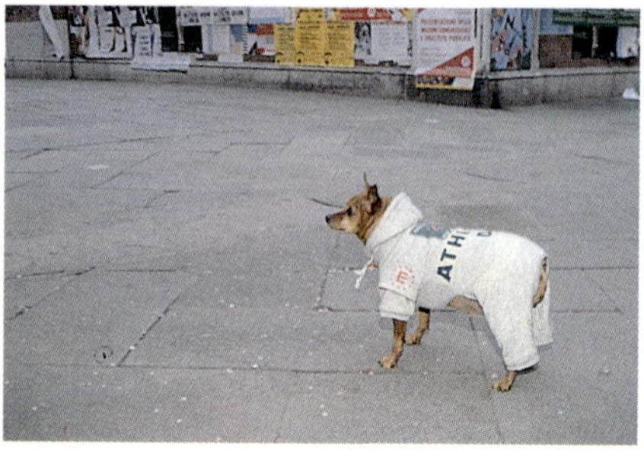

e

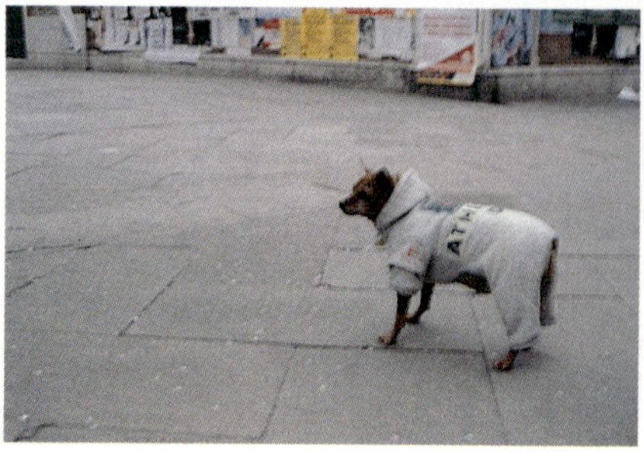

f

– Tafel IV –

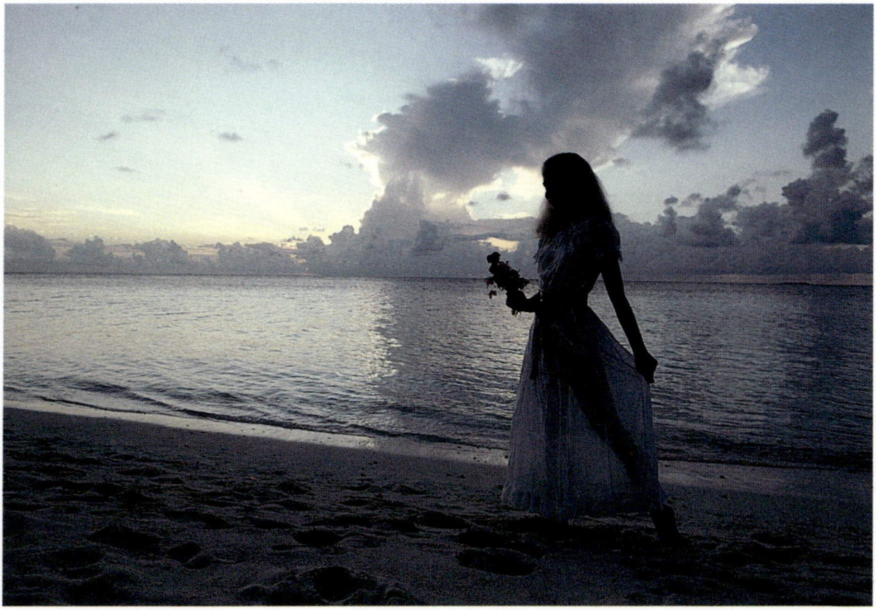

a

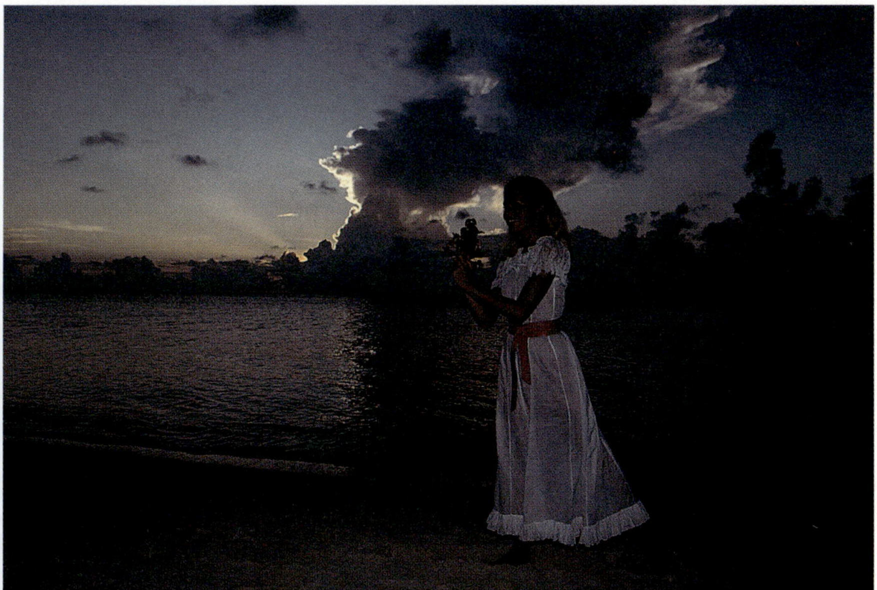

– Tafel V –

b

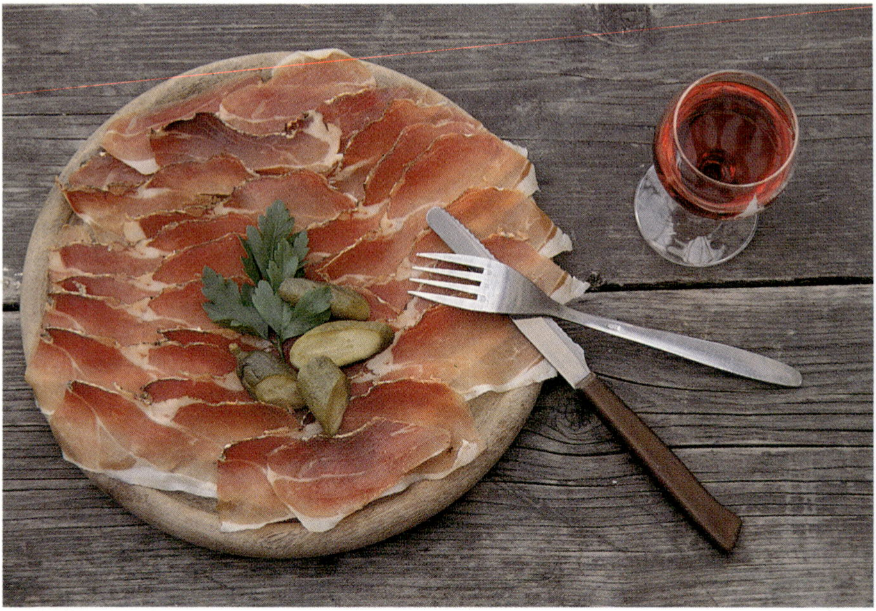

a

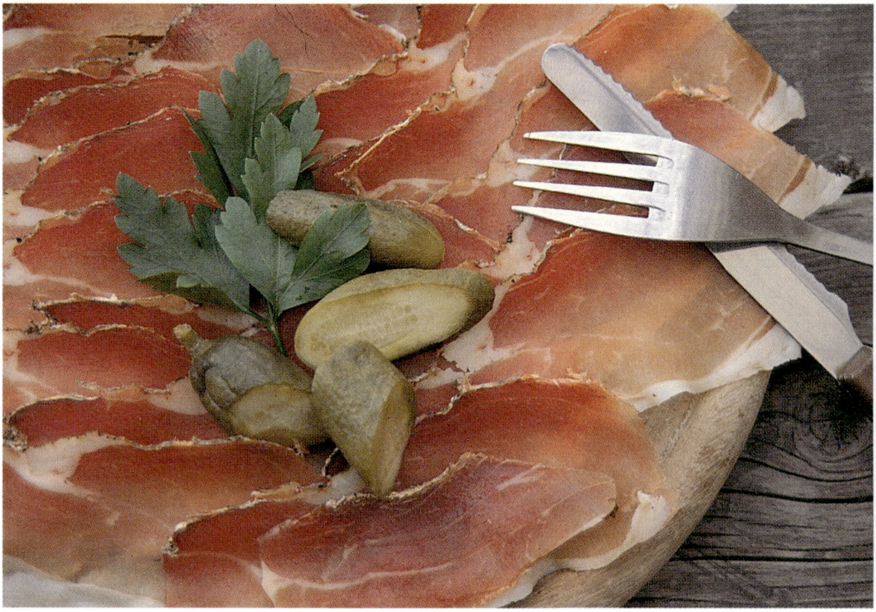

b

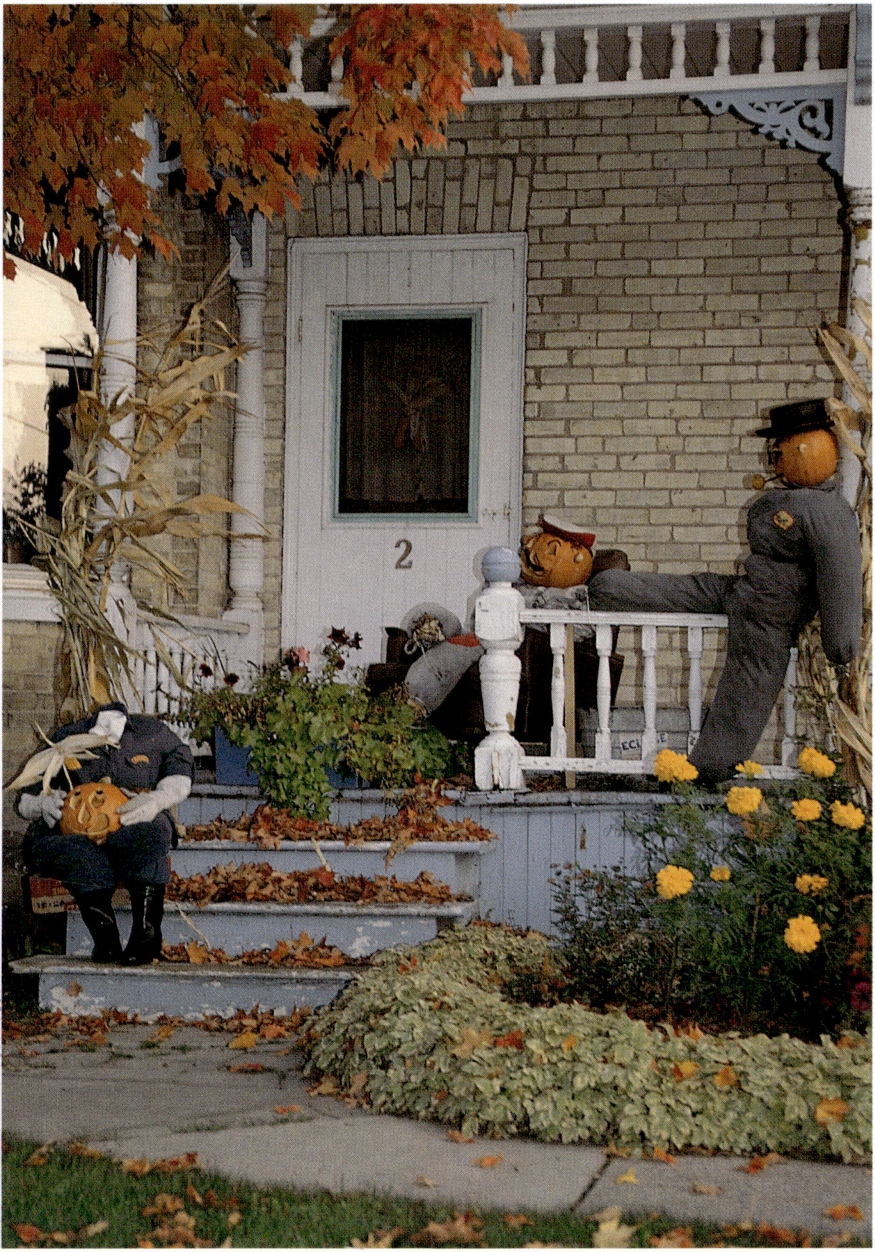

– Tafel VII –

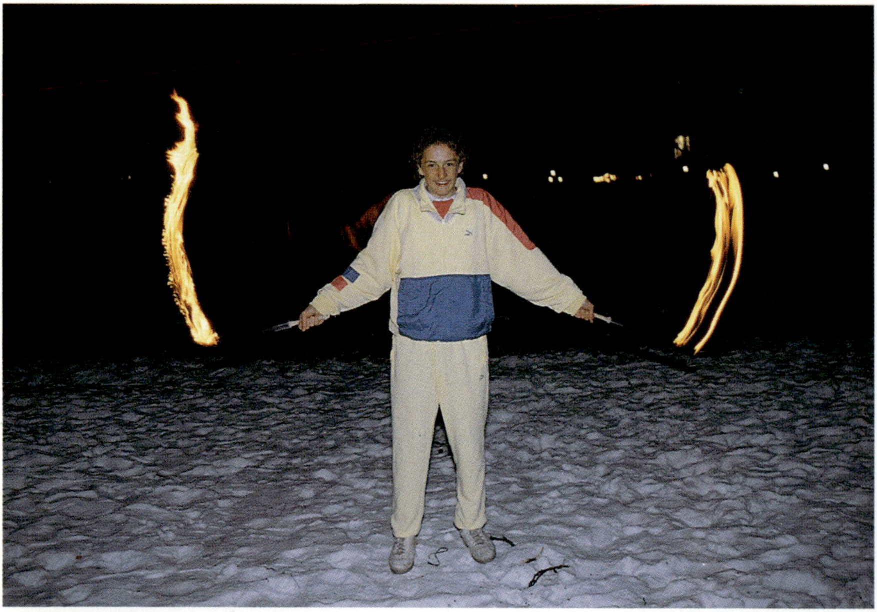

a

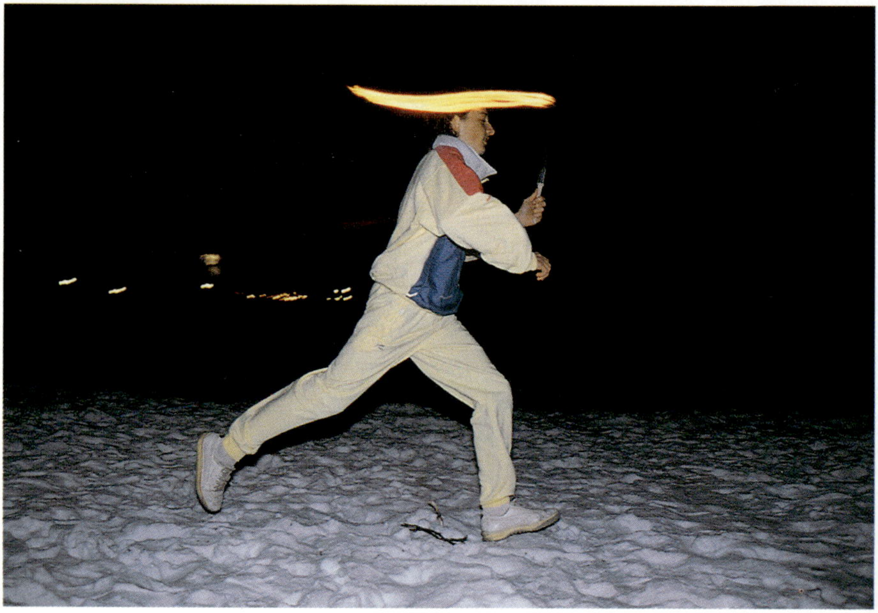

b

– Tafel VIII –

V

This ambient light exposure (picture a) rendered the subject without detail and decreased the dramatic effect of the sky. A shorter exposure captured the mood while a touch of flash (difference of three f/stops) assured that detail in the dress and face was visible. A difference of three f/stops in A (automatic sensor flash) mode was selected because very little light was reflected by the subject itself and the photographer wished to emphasize the dramatic lighting in the scene.

VI

These pictures from a lunch table in Little Italy were taken in late afternoon on a rainy day. Fill-flash improved the blue overcast light and gave the prociutto a delicious, appetizing color. The accuracy of TTL flash metering (in this case with a Minolta 7xi) assured that the colors in the telephoto exposure (picture b) matched those in the wide-angle shot (picture a).

VII

By looking carefully at this picture taken by Peter K. Burian it can be determined that fill flash was used to enhance the lighting. The brilliant sparkle and clean colors found in this Halloween "still life" could not have been achieved without flash.

VIII

Many current SLR cameras offer second shutter or rear curtain sync. This feature allows the photographer to create realistic motion blurs with flash. When using rear curtain sync, the flash is triggered as the rear shutter curtain starts to close. As illustrated in these photos, a long shutter speed captures the trail of fire, and at the end of the exposure, the flash illuminates the person.

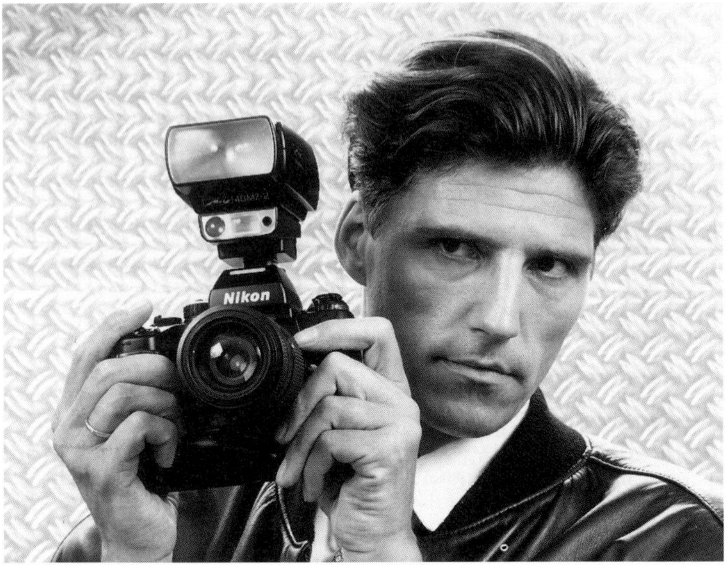

Advanced features and compatibility make the Metz Mecablitz 40 MZ 2 an excellent companion for advanced camera systems, such as the Nikon F4 shown here.

Mecablitz 40 MZ 2

This is a top-of-the-line unit in the new series of compact flash units that includes the 32 series above. These units are compatible with the SCA 3000 Adapter System. The Mecablitz 40 MZ 2 is the only flash unit in the world that combines, in one single unit, nearly every state-of-the-art feature of camera/flash technology offered by SLR camera manufacturers. Whether it is A-TTL metering offered only by Canon, wireless flash control from Minolta, or matrix metering offered by Nikon, every one of these special functions can be used with the 40 MZ 2. The performance of this unit is limited only by the camera's control functions. (For example, a Leica R6 may be used for wireless flash firing; however, the flash unit's motor-driven zoom reflector adjustment does not operate because Leica lenses do not transfer information such as focal length to the flash unit because they are still controlled entirely by mechanical means.)

A new feature of this Metz flash unit is that it uses IGBT light reg-

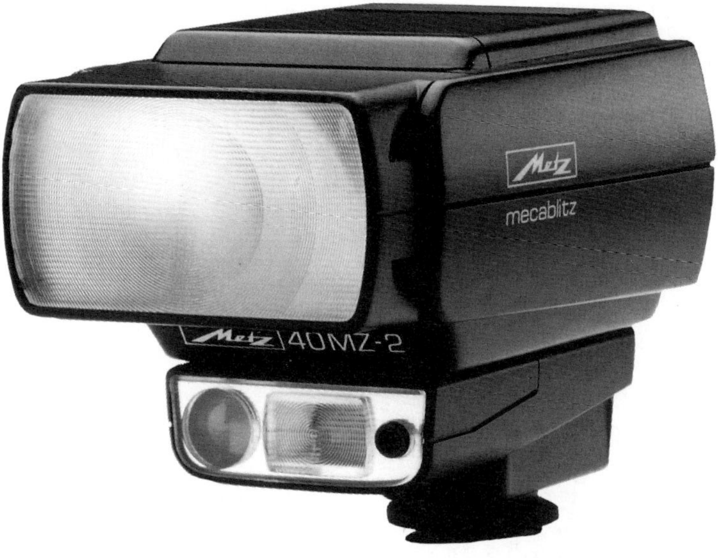

The Metz state-of-the-art 40 MZ 2 flash unit has a metric guide number of 40 at a reflector setting of 50mm at ISO 100. Other features include a motor-zoom flash head , TTL control and a built-in AF illuminator, plus it is SCA 3000 System compatible.

ulation instead of thyristor control. As a result, the flash can be controlled and activated or deactivated without delay. This is advantageous in A, automatic mode, TTL and stroboscopic mode, in the close-up range, and when using variable power output. Another feature of IGBT technology is that the flash duration can be controlled accurately enough to allow use with films as fast as ISO 6400, provided the camera has the capability to do so. In addition, this technology requires approximately one-third fewer parts, allowing more performance to be packed into such a compact design.

The 40 MZ 2 also features a well-designed LCD panel which displays flash settings such as the selected mode, including automatic mode, TTL mode, manual, stroboscopic plus, in most cases, the selected aperture and flash range. When attached to a camera using the appropriate SCA 3000 adapter, it displays camera feedback such as in automatic program mode parameters. It is also possible to store nine frequently used setting or user selected programs by simply pressing a button to lock them in.

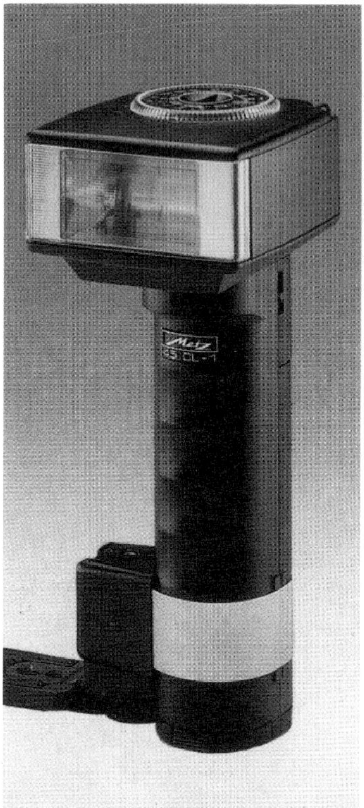

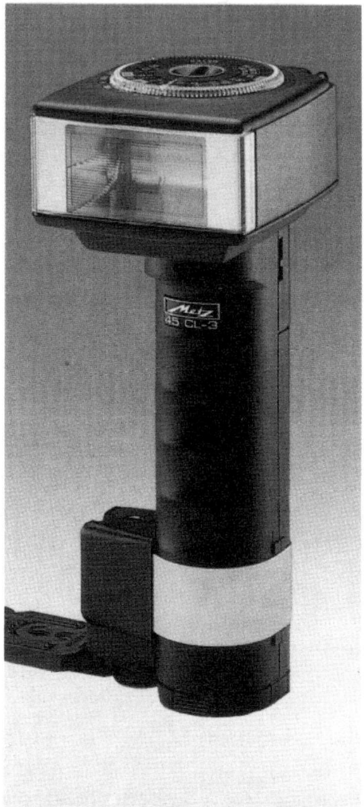

Mecablitz 45 CL 1 and CL 3 handle-mount units are the CL 4's little brothers. They're offered as "economy versions" and are ideal as back-up units without SCA Adapter hook-up. However, neither offers an LED indicator nor a secondary flash head.

Other features of the 40 MZ 2 include a power zoom flash head for 24mm, 28mm, 35mm, 50mm, 70mm and 85mm lens focal lengths, swivel/tilt reflector, 12 aperture telecomputer mode, and automatic shut-off with manual override.

Handle Mount Flash Units

Mecablitz 45 CL 1, 45 CL 3 and 45 CL 4

Today's computer-controlled Metz Mecablitz 45 CL flash units

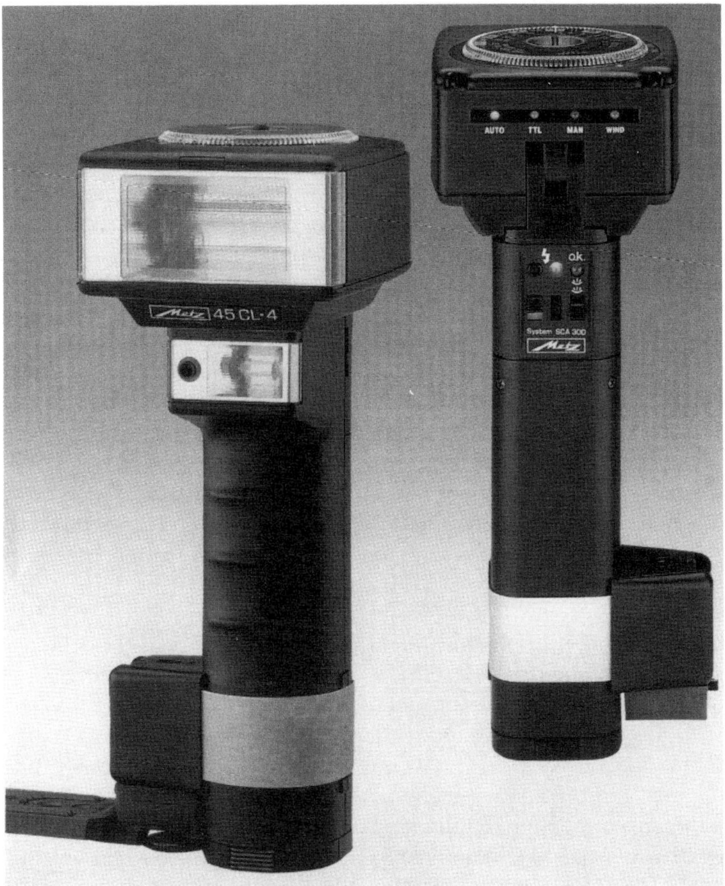

The Metz 45 CL 4 handle-mount unit offers a choice of six apertures in automatic mode; any aperture may be selected in TTL mode. It also features variable output levels and winder mode.

bear many similarities to the first Metz Mecablitz 45 CT, introduced at Photokina 1976. Though the camera models from that decade have mostly disappeared, probably many a Mecablitz of that era is still in daily use.

The 45 CL series are handle-mount flash units dimensions are: 9-1/2″ high, 4″ wide, 4-1/4″ deep (24.2 cm x 9.9 cm x 10.2 cm).

Power supply: The power supply is a rechargeable NiCd battery or a battery pack holding AA alkaline batteries. The rechargeable battery or battery pack can be changed quickly and fits in the base of the handle-mount grip. Several rechargeable batteries and at least one additional battery pack are recommended when a great number of flashes will be fired. The batteries' capacity ranges from 50 to 3600 flashes, depending on battery type, shooting distance, and the aperture used. These high flash capacities are attributable to the thyristor-controlled series circuit. The lowest value of 50 flashes per regular battery or chargeable battery refers to strictly manual firing, where the full capacitor charge is dumped with each flash (1/300 sec. flash duration). By using an AC adapter, the flash unit may be powered directly from a wall outlet. In automatic mode, the Mecablitz 45 CL 4 features a selection of six apertures, ranging from f/2.8 to f/16.

Connectors: The camera can be connected via its PC outlet, with a sync cord, or by using an SCA 300 Adapter in the camera's hot shoe. (The camera's special functions are accessible only with synchronization via the SCA Adapter.)

The Quadrolight reflector: The 45 series reflector covers the image angle of a 35mm lens for 35mm cameras. The angle of illumination can be enlarged to 28mm with a wide-angle attachment supplied with the flash. This will reduce the guide number. For bounce illumination, the flash head can be rotated horizontally through 360 degrees and pivoted vertically by 90 degrees, in six fixed positions. When using bounce illumination, the secondary flash head located directly beneath the main flash head can be activated to provide fill light. This aims 15% of the total light directly at the subject, while the remaining 85% provides soft, indirect light.

Flash verification: Many inexperienced photographers forget - particularly when using bounce flash - that there is a maximum shooting distance. However, the Mecablitz will detect this distance and signal if light output is sufficient. The Flash Verification indicator on the flash unit will signal that the amount of light was adequate for correct exposure. The photographer may rely on this verification with normal subjects, but unusually light or dark subjects require manual correction. The top of the Quadrolight reflector has a well laid out adjustment panel. The photographer may refer to this for maximum shooting distance, independent of the selected mode.

Shooting range: TTL flash metering, even using a wide-angle diffuser, requires slightly more attention. The internal aperture data should line up with the indicated maximum shooting distance when the functions set are TTL and computerized mode. However, the maximum shooting distance is not necessarily the distance between camera and subject but instead is the distance which must be traveled by the light from the flash. That is, the distance equals the distance from the flash to the reflective surface combined with the distance from that surface to the subject. With bounce flash this path is clearly longer and this must be considered when choosing the aperture.

Manual mode: In addition to the modes mentioned so far, the adjustment panel at the top of the flash head also has a setting marked "M" for manual adjustment or M 1/2 and M 1/4 for reduced flash output. An output reduction may also be achieved with higher flash speeds. An adjustment to the yellow W reduces the output as low as 1/40, resulting in a guide number of 6 meter (21 feet) at ISO 100 (GN factor = 0.15) and a flash duration of approximately 1/10,000 sec. This allows the 45 CL 4 to fire 2 flashes per second with the use of a rechargeable battery. Professional photographers using ISO 400 (specifically black and white) material may work with an aperture of f/4 at 10.5 feet (3.5 m) and a guide number of 49 feet (14 m), which is highly acceptable.

Operating mode indicators: An array of control indicators on the opposite side of the reflector is equally important; these indicators clearly signal the selected operating mode, namely, green for automatic, orange for TTL-SCA, red for manual and yellow for winder mode.

Close-up range: When pictures are taken in the close-up range, the minimum distance must be noted when using a Metz handle-mount unit. This distance is approximately 10% of the maximum shooting distance. If photos are taken at closer distances, images will be overexposed. However, minimum shooting distances may

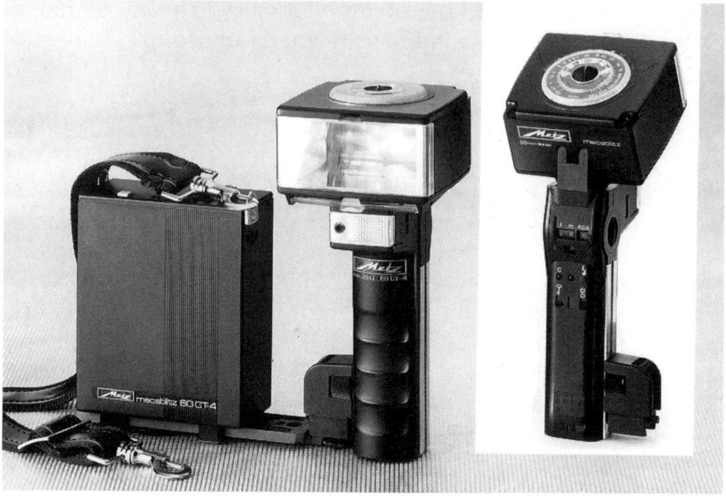

The Metz Mecablitz 60 CT 4 is the "powerhouse" of the Metz flash system. Its external battery allows for extremely fast recycling times. Advanced features like TTL flash mode and SCA 300 system compatibility make it a more versatile flash unit.

be reduced by outwitting the flash unit. The light-absorbing diffuser screen may be used when taking pictures in the close-up range with the handle-mount unit. Any other material, such as a tissue or pocket handkerchief may also be used to reduce the light output. An additional advantage is pleasant, soft illumination.

Accessories: The comprehensive line of accessories are covered in detail later in this chapter. At this point, it will only be mentioned that filter kits for coloring light and light reduction, a tele attachment and a variety of power sources are a few of the available accessories for 45 series flash units.

Mecablitz 60 CT 1 and 60 CT 4

These professional Mecablitz units with high guide number have proven themselves a thousand times over in daily use. The Mecablitz 60 CT 1 is considered an economy version however, it is still an excellent choice for many applications. After all, many tasks do not absolutely require the added special features of the Mecablitz 60 CT 4.

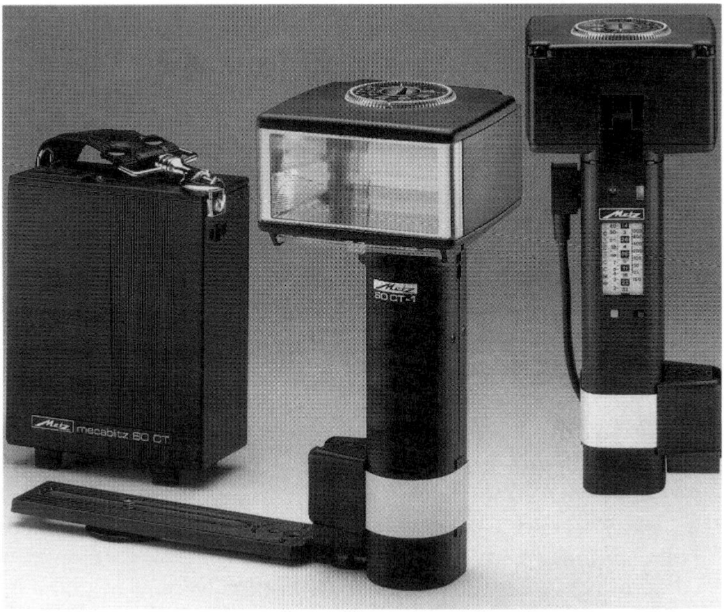

The Metz 60 CT 1 is a more basic flash unit than the 60 CT 4. Although it offers the same light output, it lacks more sophisticated functions like TTL flash mode and SCA adaptor control.

Mecablitz 60 CT 1 and CT 4 are high-quality, high-performance units with a metric guide number of 60 (210 in feet), which gives them double the light output of GN 45 handle-mount units.

SCA compatibility: Until the end of 1992, 60 series units were still integrated in the SCA 500 Adapter System. Now the 60 CT 4 has all of the capabilities of the SCA 300 Adapter System. It may even be used with the red-light cable of the SCA 3000 Adapter System to support automatic focusing of AF cameras by Canon, Minolta, Nikon and Pentax from approximately 18 inches (45 cm) to at least 27 feet (9 m).

Power sources: 60 series units come in two pieces: a handle grip ("potato masher") holding only the flash components and a separate power pack holding NiCd or chargeable Dryfit (lead acid) batteries. One charge of the maintenance-free Dryfit battery produces between 150 and 4,500 flashes. The N 23 AC Adapter offers an unlimited number of flashes with 60 series as well as 45 series handle-mount units, wherever a standard 120V outlet is available.

Verifying charge condition: Not all Metz flash units offer automatic shut off. This requires the understanding that 5 to 6 minutes of flash readiness mode use up as much power as one full flash. Professional photographers often work with several rechargeable NiCd battery sets simultaneously, so freshly charged batteries are always available. It is also important to remember that, because of self-discharge, NiCd batteries must be recharged approximately every 3 months if not used.

Professional features: The remaining features of these units are as professional as the power supply. Recycling times range between 0.25 and 5 seconds. Additional features of professional flash units include a permanently mounted wide-angle diffuser, 8 computerized apertures (f/2 to f/22), a lock against inadvertent resetting of film speed and aperture, 5 light output levels and a motor-driven flash output for up to 5 exposures per second.

Use care to avoid overheating: When a series of continuous flash exposures of more than 30 successive flashes at full light output (i.e., manual or automatic mode) is taken, the flash may overheat dangerously. Therefore, "continuous mode" should include at least a 30 second break between individual flash runs. "Discontinuous mode" should include a break of at least 4 minutes after ten flash exposures have been taken (with the shortest recycling time).

Which Metz Flash is Best?

This question is not always easily answered. On one hand, you want to avoid adding unnecessary equipment, but on the other hand, a flash unit should offer maximum firing convenience and power.

While it used to be true that the basic choice was between a compact or a handle-mount unit, this is no longer so important.

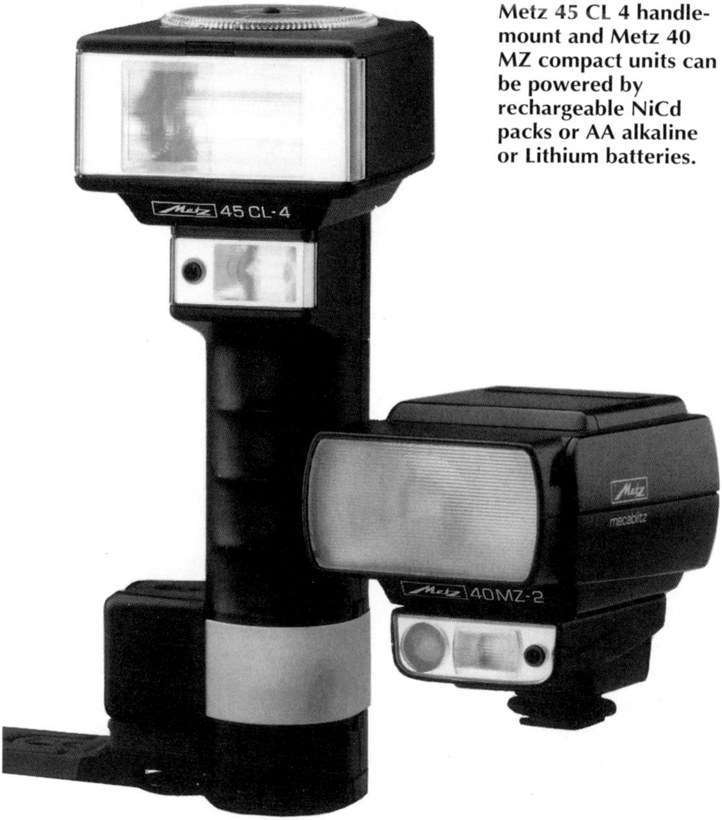

Metz 45 CL 4 handle-mount and Metz 40 MZ compact units can be powered by rechargeable NiCd packs or AA alkaline or Lithium batteries.

For example, the difference between the guide numbers of a compact unit such as the Mecablitz 40 MZ 2 and the handle-mount 45 CL unit is hardly worth mentioning.

By attaching an accessory handle or power grip, all SCA 300 and SCA 3000 compact units can easily be converted into handle-mount units. As a result, these units become handier for some professional applications. In addition, the batteries in the grip provide power for three times as many flashes and quicker recycling times.

There are obvious advantages of handle-mount flash units which can also be operated from an AC power source via accessories. This feature appeals to photographers who use them in the

The 45 series units offer interchangeable battery holders for quick battery changes whether using NiCds or conventional alkaline batteries.

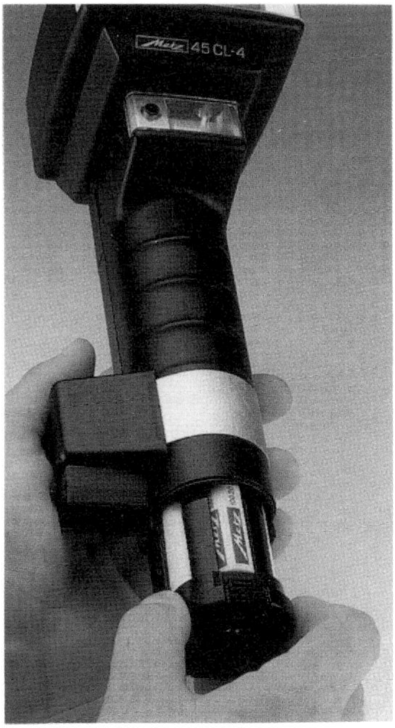

studio. In addition, these units are engineered for greater mechanical and electrical stress. And, because it is assumed that the photographer is familiar with flash technology, there are no technical gimmicks.

Metz Power Options

Metz flash units are designed to work off of a variety of power supplies from alkaline batteries to AC power. Beginning with battery operation, there are many choices in terms of quality and performance.

Zinc carbon batteries: An inexpensive solution is offered by zinc carbon batteries which, although not recommended, provide enough power for one or two rolls of film. Such batteries should be used only when nothing else is available.

Alkaline batteries: The most popular battery choice, alkaline batteries have a much greater capacity and longer life than the zinc carbons mentioned above. Besides being available at your Metz photo dealer, AA alkaline batteries are also in abundant supply at any supermarket or convenience store.

Lithium batteries: Even longer life is offered by lithium batteries, which now can be used with a number of flash units. They have double the capacity of alkaline batteries, allowing a greater maximum number of flashes. Lithium batteries have built-in overload protection which prevents overheating. If many flashes are fired within a short time, the overload protection may be activated and flash recycling times may become very long. A fast battery change, allowing the battery to cool outside the flash unit, may help, otherwise the flash must be switched off until the batteries have cooled.

Rechargeable Batteries

These are environmentally "friendly." There are the familiar NiCd (nickel-cadmium) rechargeable batteries and also Dryfit, rechargeable lead-acid batteries (basically, a smaller version of an automobile battery).

Dryfit batteries: These batteries are supplied as a separate power pack and used with the 60 series handle-mount flash units. These modern, gas-tight rechargeable lead-acid batteries are a heavy-duty power storage system, offering up to 4,500 flashes per charge. Although the charging time is comparatively long, Dryfit batteries have an exceptionally low rate of spontaneous discharge. Batteries can be stored up to six months without requiring recharging.

NiCd ("Nicad") batteries: Because nickel-cadmium batteries exhibit higher power-carrying capacity than alkaline batteries, they allow faster flash recycling times and are suitable at lower temperatures. Their overall capacity, however, is lower and therefore they last only for approximately 1/2 of the number of flashes compared with Dryfit batteries. Only freshly charged NiCd batteries should be used. Theoretically, modern NiCd batteries are capable of up to 1,000 charging cycles when used with a good charging unit. Also they may be a sensible alternative from an economical, as well as ecological, viewpoint. In practice, however, the capacity of NiCd batteries is often reduced significantly due to the so-called "memory effect." After having been used about 10 to 20 times or after extended non-use the battery may hold less and less charged energy.

Multiple AC adapter: Metz also offers the Multiple AC power adapter for use with 45 and 60 series professional flash units. This allows one 60 series or two 45 series flash units to be used with the unlimited power of a wall outlet. It is an excellent accessory for photographers using Metz units in the studio.

Power source considerations: Photographers who take many flash pictures should consider using a flash unit that accepts rechargeable batteries as the power source, because one rechargeable battery pack can be charged while a second one is in use. This is the reason that rechargeable batteries are a top choice of professional Metz users.

Power-related Flash Features

Ready lamp: The capacitor must be recharged after each flash. When the capacitor reaches a sufficient charge (the standard is 75% of full charge), a "flash ready" lamp or LED on the flash unit will light up. Some cameras have a flash ready indicator in the viewfinder, and some also use an audible signal to indicate flash readiness.

Flash verification indicator: This indicator on the flash unit blinks to signal that the flash has produced sufficient light for correct exposure. You can also use the "OK" indicator by making a test flash to check whether the flash will provide enough light and whether the subject is within the flash shooting range.

Battery tester: Compact flash units have a battery tester. Pushing the test button indicates whether the remaining battery capacity is sufficient. However, this indicator works only with alkaline batteries. Generally, battery warning indicators are more effective.

Battery warning indicator: This is a fairly recent addition to Metz flash units, available only with the Mecablitz 40 MZ 2. It produces a visual and audible warning signal when the battery capacity is low. (A battery is considered exhausted when charging the flash unit takes more than 60 seconds.)

Automatic shut-off: The automatic shut-off prevents the unnecessary use of power if you forget to switch off the unit when not in use. All but the most basic Metz compact flash units have this feature. The Mecablitz 40 MZ 2 offers the option of setting the unit to the "clock" symbol. The unit will switch off automatically when it has not been fired for 10 minutes but will retain the last settings you were using, so they are still available when the flash is switched back on.

Key-function: This feature locks in the flash settings to prevent inadvertent resetting.

Flash Head Movements

Nearly all flash units today have a tilting and rotating flash head that allows you to adjust the reflector for bounce flash and for close-up photos. Some flash units have downward tilting flash heads to compensate for parallax in the close-up range.

Zoom flash head: With many Metz flash units, you can also adjust the angle of illumination to match the focal length of the lens in use. This provides optimum utilization of the light from the flash and makes the most of the available battery power. The flash head should offer at least a manual zoom adjustment; an automatic zoom adjustment is better. This adjustment guarantees, for example, that the flash unit's illumination will cover the full picture area when a wide-angle lens is used, such as a 28mm lens on a 35mm camera.

There are a few special cases when it makes sense to adjust the zoom setting manually. One example is when using fill flash to take a picture of a person in the foreground, with a landscape in the background, using a wide-angle lens on the camera. If you set the flash reflector to a tele setting, so the flash illumination covers just the person, you will minimize the drain on the batteries and avoid a possible overexposure of the portrait subject.

Metz Flash Modes

Not every flash unit is compatible with all the advanced flash technology which has been developed in recent years. Metz has constantly upgraded their flash units as camera manufacturers update.

Many of the available functions are called different names by the various camera manufacturers. Sophisticated flash functions are camera dependant with communication between flash and camera, via the appropriate SCA adapter, required for proper performance (see Chapter 2 on the SCA system). Flash units cannot perform functions not offered by the camera.

Automatic flash mode: Normal automatic flash mode is the simplest yet one of the most effective ways of metering and controlling the flash. A built-in photocell, also known as a Metz "telecomputer," measures the flash light reflected by the subject. This photocell is connected to a circuit that automatically shuts off power to the flash tube as soon as the amount of light required for a correct exposure has been detected. The best measurement is provided when the light-to-dark ratio in the subject is balanced. With Metz flash units, the sensitivity of the telecomputer may be adjusted for different aperture values. The more aperture adjustments, the better, particularly when fill flash is used and the amount of flash must be adjusted precisely.

TTL flash mode: Most of today's 35mm cameras and many medium-format cameras offer TTL-OTF flash metering. This stands for Through The Lens-Off The Film. In TTL mode and automatic fill flash mode, the light coming through the lens and hitting the film is measured by a sensor inside the camera. The flash exposure is controlled through this sensor and a thyristor circuit which shuts off the flash tube when sufficient light has been measured. Thus, the flash unit's output is controlled by the camera's automatic exposure control, by means of the SCA adapter.

A-TTL flash mode: In this flash mode, a pre-flash determines distance and exposure parameters. The camera's electronic system uses these parameters to automatically determine the required shutter speed/aperture combination and to control the output of the flash unit. Only Canon EOS cameras use this system.

Program mode: Settings for up to nine different flash programs can be entered into the flash unit's memory by the user.

Manual flash mode: This is the basic flash mode in which the flash unit's full output is used. Exposure is controlled by different lens aperture settings based on the guide number for a given subject distance.

Winder mode: This mode permits the flash unit to fire two exposures per second. Flash recycling time is shortened by reducing the power output.

Motor-drive mode: This mode is basically similar to winder mode, but the flash will allow up to five exposures per second. Currently, only the big handle-mount Mecablitz 60 CT 1 and 4, and the Mecablitz 40 MZ 2, the star among the Metz compact units, have this capability.

Stroboscopic flash mode: Although many photographers incorrectly call any electronic flash unit a "strobe," the correct meaning of this term refers to a flash unit that provides rapidly repeated flashes. The Mecablitz 40 MZ 2 is the only Metz flash unit that can be used for stroboscopic exposures. This "lightning" mode permits multiple flash exposures on a single frame of film, a technique which is especially useful for motion studies and special effects. In this mode the power consumption is particularly high and new batteries, an AC adapter or a freshly charged battery pack should be used.

Remote wireless TTL flash control mode: The Metz TTL remote control allows wireless flash operation of several flash units independent of the camera or camera system. This system operates by means of coded infrared pulses sent from the master flash to the slave units. Metz offers this flash technology for Minolta xi and si cameras Minolta offers this feature with its newest generation flash units.

The Minolta 5400-xi programmed flash unit may be used in conjunction with a Metz Mecablitz 40 MZ 2. Likewise, the built-in Minolta flash unit is compatible with the Metz 40 MZ 2 and can utilize Minolta's exposure control system.

Partial light output mode: In this mode the flash output can be adjusted from 1/1 to 1/256, depending on the model. In the latter case, the increments are 1/3 of a stop in size, which is important when the flash output must be precisely controlled. This allows total control over aperture selection. Also, "power ratio" control of flash light output allows faster recycling and may be used in all flash modes except the fully programmed automatic and remote wireless TTL flash modes.

AF illuminator mode: Metz makes an SCA autofocus adapter which can be placed between the adapter foot and the flash unit. This adapter provides auxiliary red light for autofocusing when photographing in low-light or low-contrast conditions. This adapter is not needed with the newer Metz flash units, which have the AF auxiliary light built in.

Metz Mecablitz Flash Accessories

Metz provides a number of special accessories to meet photographers' specific needs. For example, to make sure your flash unit is always ready for use, you may want additional rechargeable batteries or an automatic charger. For flash photography at extended distances, the Metz tele attachment for handle-mount flash units concentrates the light and almost doubles the maximum range of the flash unit.

The product line includes five groups of accessories:

1. Accessories to facilitate handling of the camera and flash unit.
2. Accessories for lighting in specific picture-taking situations.
3. Power supply accessories.
4. Accessories that enhance the combined use of several flash units.
5. Accessories for automatic focusing.

Accessories for Easier Handling

In some cases, the combination of camera and handle-mount flash unit can become unwieldy and may even make camera handling and operation inconvenient. These Metz accessories help solve that problem.

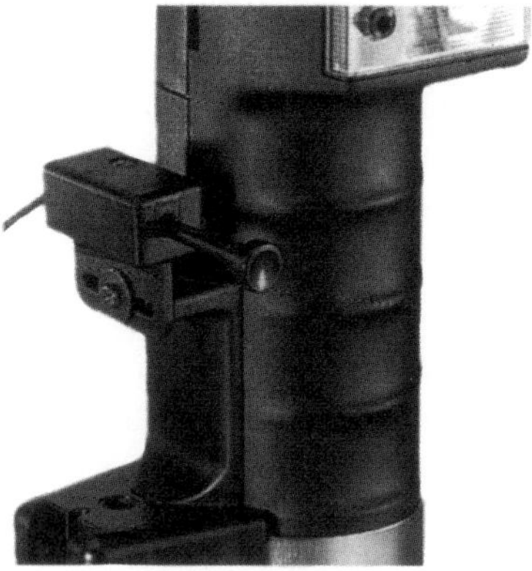

Camera cable releases are available to attach to Metz handle-mount flash units and the Power Grip G 15.

Camera cable release: The camera cable release can be used with model 45 and 60 handle-mount units or with the Metz Power Grips. It allows convenient shutter tripping with one hand on the handle mount and the other under the lens.

Camera Cable Release 45-26 - for Mecablitz 45 and 60 CT 1
Camera Cable Release 60-20 - for Power Grip G 15 and Mecablitz 60 CT 4

Electronic camera release: Many electronically controlled cameras require an electronic camera release instead of a mechanical one, and this release makes it convenient to trip the shutter from the flash handle.
Electronic Camera Release 45-25 - for Mecablitz 45 and 60 CT 1
Electronic Camera Release 60-25 - for Mecablitz 60 CT 4

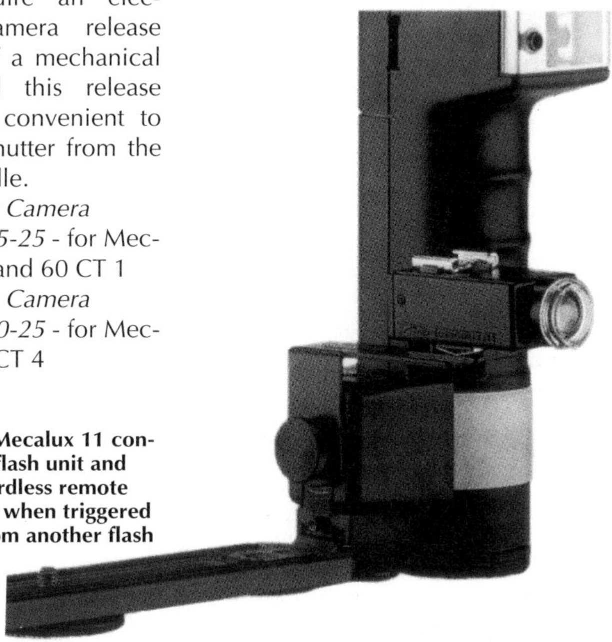

The Metz Mecalux 11 connects to a flash unit and permits cordless remote flash firing when triggered by light from another flash unit.

Mecalux 11: This is a highly sensitive white light slave that fires the attached flash unit when it detects the flash from another unit. It operates with both manually controlled and automatic flash units.

Camera platform: This accessory is recommended for mounting medium-format cameras securely on the Metz camera bracket.

Bracket adapter: Both adjustable and fixed adapters are available to prevent parallax when taking close-up shots with handle-mount flash units. The adapter positions the flash reflector approximately 6 inches (15 cm) lower than usual, at the level of the camera lens.
Bracket Adapter 60-28 – Adjustable
Bracket Adapter 45-35 – Fixed

The adjustable Flash Bracket Adapter 60-28 eliminates parallax problems in close-up photography.

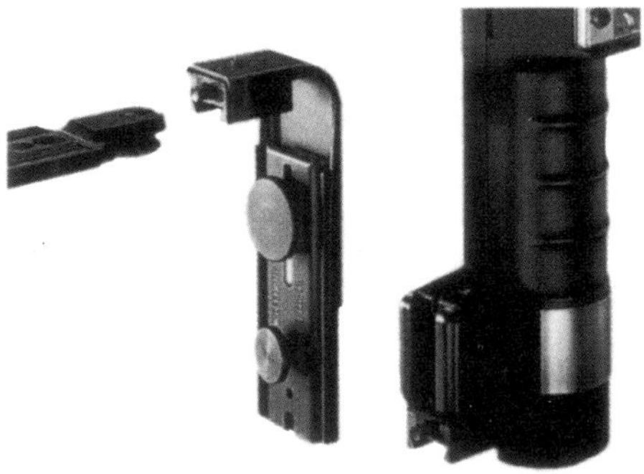

Accessories for Optimum Lighting
These accessories help provide the best lighting in the telephoto and wide-angle ranges.

Wide-angle attachment: Wide-angle attachments are sold with or built into most Mecablitz flash units to increase their coverage when using a wide-angle lens. The 60 CT has a built-in wide-angle diffuser; the reflector on the Mecablitz 40 MZ 2 can be adjusted for 24mm super wide-angle coverage.

Tele attachment: All Mecablitz 45 and 60 flash units and older Mecatwin handle-mount units, can be used with this accessory which effectively concentrates the flash beam for telephoto pictures; focal lengths of 120mm and greater with a 35mm camera.

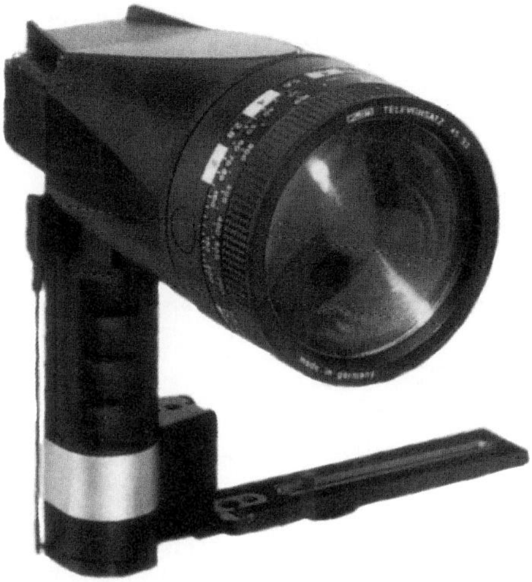

A Tele-attachment concentrates the flash into a narrow beam for use with focal lengths of 120mm and greater. It is ideal for use in nature photography and for sports photography when flash is permitted.

The attachment's fresnel lens narrows the flash beam to cover 11 degrees vertically and 19 degrees horizontally, which nearly doubles the maximum flash range. Precise alignment is required and is facilitated with a bracket adapter.

This attachment is particularly effective for long-range animal photography and for sports events and allows TTL flash metering. If TTL metering is not available with your camera and flash unit, the Mecamat Universal Sensor can provide automatic exposure control by setting it to a measuring angle of 12 degrees. The light can easily be filtered by inserting colored gels or other filter material into the adapter. For example, you can use an infrared-transmitting filter to take pictures on infrared film using almost invisible infrared flashes.

Telephoto Attachment 45-33 - for Mecablitz 45 series and Mecatwin 60-40

Telephoto Attachment 60-42 - for Mecablitz 60 CT 1 and CT 4

Reflectors: These permit soft, indirect lighting. These reflectors fit Metz handle-mount flash units and are supplied with appropriate holders.

Reflector 32-73 - for Mecablitz 28 CT 5 and 32 CT 7

Reflector 32-75 - for Mecablitz 32 Z series

Reflector 40-23 - for Mecablitz 40 MZ 2

Reflector 60-33 - for Mecablitz 45 and 60

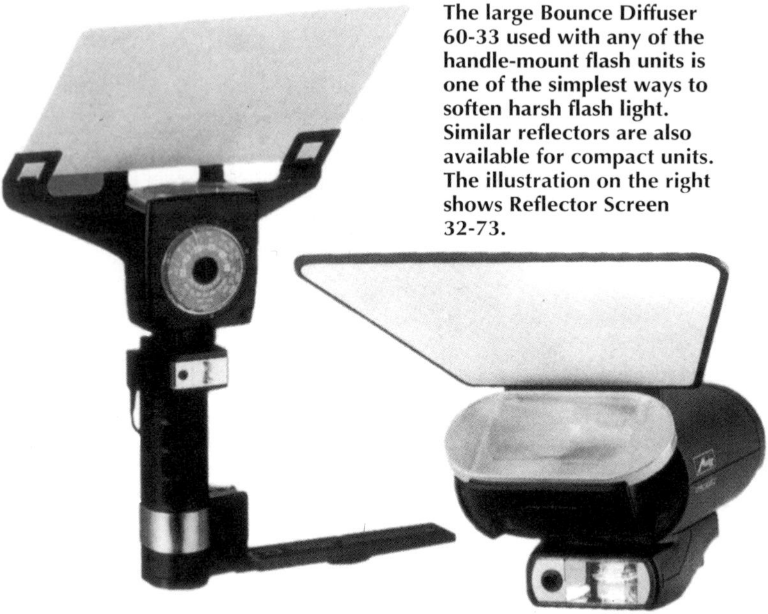

The large Bounce Diffuser 60-33 used with any of the handle-mount flash units is one of the simplest ways to soften harsh flash light. Similar reflectors are also available for compact units. The illustration on the right shows Reflector Screen 32-73.

Filter kits: Two types of filter kits are available: neutral density filters, for light reduction, especially useful with the TTL Multi-connector and several SCA flash units, and colored filters, for

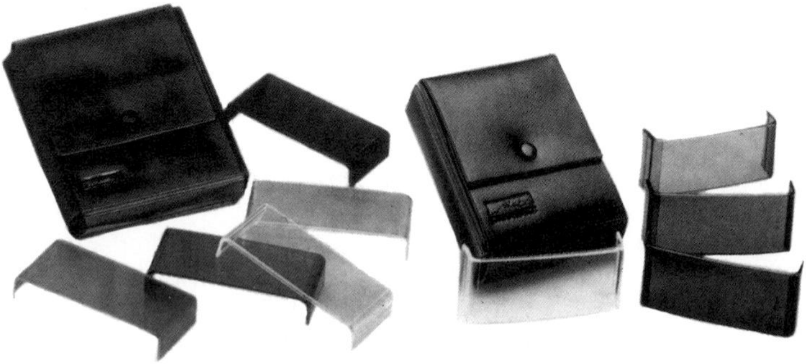

Metz color filter kits are designed for creative use of color with flash photography. A set of light-reducing filters is also available. Both sets come with a protective case.

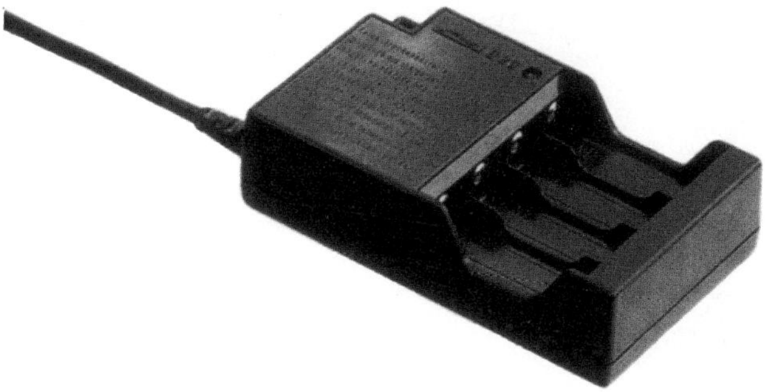

The B-28 battery charger can be used to charge four individual rechargeable NiCd batteries at one time.

creative lighting effects. This set includes a transparent filter holder and yellow, green, blue and red filters.

Power Supply Accessories
Battery Charger B 28: This unit charges four NiCd batteries.

Auto Battery Connecting Cable A 17: This connecting cable is used with the B 28 charger and plugs into a car's cigarette lighter for recharging NiCd batteries from a 12V DC automobile battery.

NC-Charge Set B 45: This charger and battery set converts a Mecablitz 45 series flash from regular battery operation to rechargeable NiCd battery operation.

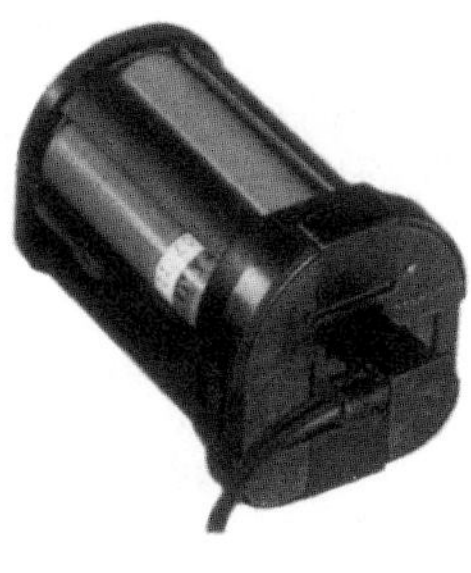

The NiCd Set B 45 includes charger and batteries for use with 45 CL series flash units.

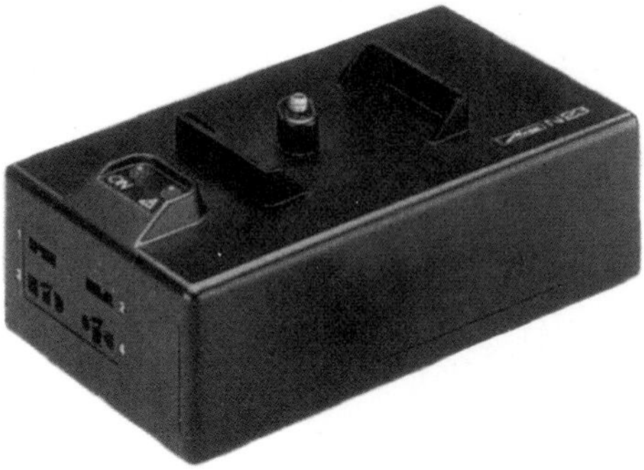

The N 23 AC adapter is designed to operate 45 and 60 handle-mount flash units with power from a standard wall outlet. This works well when fast recycling times are desired and limited movement does not present a problem.

AC Adapter N 23: Powers one Mecablitz 60 or two 45 series flash units directly from a 120V AC outlet and provides fast recycling times. Appropriate flash connection cord is required.

AC Adapter N 22: Allows a single 45 series flash unit to operate from a 120V AC outlet.

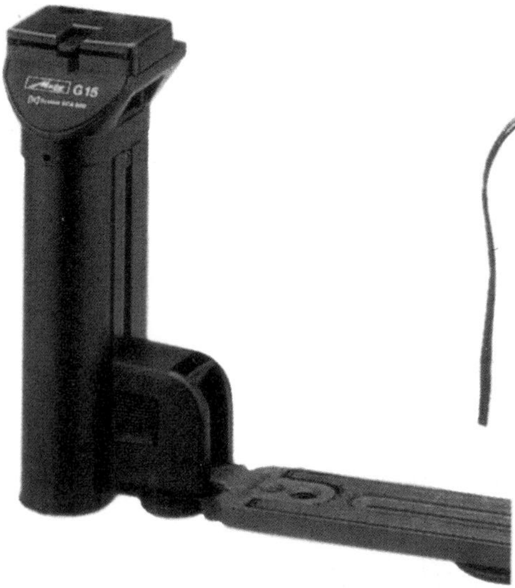

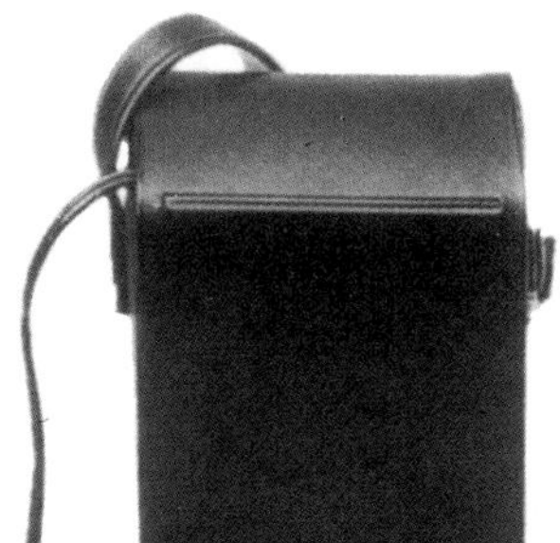

The Metz Power Grip (left) adds battery power and a convenient handle to Metz compact flash units. Power Pack 45-45 (right) can be used with handle-mount flash units to triple flash capacity while reducing recycling time.

Power Pack 45-45: This power pack works with handle-mount flash units to triple the flash capacity and significantly reduce recycling times.

Power Grips G 15 and G 16: Mecablitz Power Grips convert Metz compact flash units into handle-mount flash units and increase their flash capacity by at least three times.
Power Grip G 15 - for SCA 300 System flash units.
Power Grip G 16 - for SCA 3000 System flash units.

Accessories for Combining Several Flash Units

TTL Multiconnector SCA 305 A: This universal distribution system controls up to three interconnected SCA flash units by means of the camera's TTL flash metering system. As many as seven flash units can be controlled by combining several TTL Multiconnectors.

SCA 305 A Extension cable: Extension cable for the TTL Multiconnector SCA 305 A for off-camera flash exposures; connects the flash unit and SCA adapter. Coiled cords (SCA 307 and SCA 3007).

Sync cords: Regular extension sync cords are also available to attach to the camera's PC outlet. Available in lengths of 3 feet and 15 feet or 3.75 feet for the CT 60.

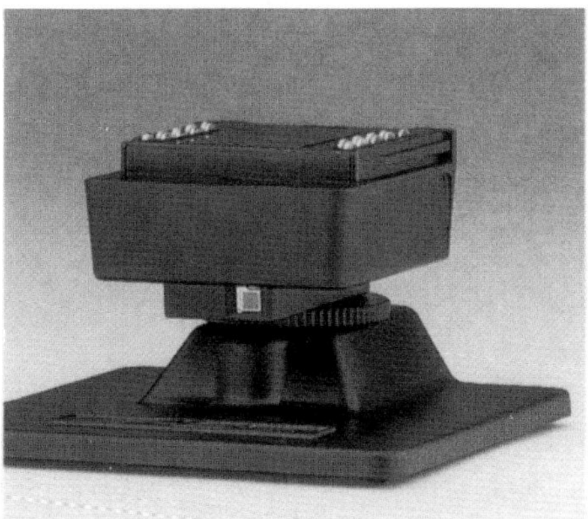

SCA 3080 Slave Adapter with accessory foot stand.

Accessories for Automatic Focusing

Mecamat Sensor: An ideal external sensor for Mecablitz 45 CL 3 and 4 units. Offers as many as 11 aperture settings, 7 partial light output settings for fixed flash durations, an integrated flash readiness indicator, and a metering-angle adjustment to switch between angles of 25 degrees and 12 degrees. Ideal for macro and telephoto applications.

Slave Adapter 3080: With a Mecablitz 40 MZ 2 and wireless TTL flash metering, this adaptor allows wireless control of the off-camera flash unit.

Advanced Metz Flash Techniques

Creative Use of Light

It is thanks to light that there are any photographic subjects at all. And it is thanks to light that there are colors, because they are a function of light. Without light, everything is black and every object, colorless.

This may appear to be self-evident, but it should be taken literally. It means, for example, that in pitch darkness a green tree is not green, it is colorless, or black. The green color of the tree reappears only when light is cast on it. And since color is created by light, any object, any photographic subject, may change its color with a change of light. More precisely, the color of the light (its color temperature) changes.

Color itself is pure light. Isaac Newton was the first to prove this, and any photographer can do so each time you take a picture with electronic flash — your "personal sun" — using it to cast additional light on the subject and hence adding more color to the image.

By taking a careful look at your pictures, you may find that frequently it was not so important what was photographed, but instead when, and how, and at what time of day the picture was taken, and how the light in the photograph was reflected. The setting and the mood created by the light may arouse the viewer's interest more than the subject itself. Your photographs will benefit when you learn to recognize, to consider, and to utilize these effects.

Light, including flash, is the most underrated creative tool. Apart from the fact that a subject is visible only because of light, Andreas Feininger, one of the most famous American photographers, believes that light has three additional functions:

1. It is responsible for the illusion of space and depth.
2. It creates moods.
3. It forms graphic patterns or simple light/dark patterns.

In addition, these three functions of light can be manipulated creatively by adjusting the intensity, the color, the angle of incidence, the contrast, and the formation of shadows.

Light comes in varied forms: radiant, direct, reflected, diffuse, shadowless, filtered, polarized, natural, artificial and continuous light, as well as light emitted by a point source or by a diffuse source with a large area. Creative photographers mix and combine all these forms and types of light, and thus produce unlimited variations of illumination. This wealth of options can be mastered only by persistently experimenting and testing.

You should be familiar with the basics of lighting in order to evaluate both subject and lighting condition and take optimum advantage of the situation. To do this, you must consciously view and evaluate the existing light. An untrained eye will not notice the composition of light but will notice only the obvious effects, such as whether there is enough light for reading, whether the sun is shining into the lens, or the like. This is not adequate for creative photography. You must learn to understand and evaluate the intensity, composition and direction of light. Only then can you use "your light" creatively.

Light Incidence

There are four main directions for incident light:

1. Front light
2. Side light at a 45 degree angle
3. Side light at a 90 degree angle
4. Backlight

By using these variations of incident light you can modify the creative composition, the surface rendition, and the distribution of light and shadows, and can also emphasize and enhance the appearance of a subject in front of a background.

Lighting effects are most pronounced when the light is concentrated and directional, as with bright sunlight or with direct flash. When the light becomes softer - sunlight diffused by clouds, or artificial light with the use of a reflector or diffuser -the effect of the light becomes less pronounced.

The most important rule to understand when dealing with light is that the "hardness" or "softness" of the light on a subject is determined by the apparent size of the light source as seen from the subject's position. Thus, a direct flash is always relatively harsh, since the flash tube is quite small and operates almost as a point source (the harshest type of light). Diffusers, soft boxes, reflectors, and similar devices are simply intended to increase the apparent size of the light source and thereby to soften it. The softest light of all is from an overcast sky, a situation in which the apparent size of the light source is nearly infinite. Remembering this one rule about the apparent size of the light source will help you create the type of lighting you want for any subject.

Front Light

Front lighting means the light source is at your back or is mounted on your camera. Front lighting illuminates the subject from the photographer's direction, and therefore creates hardly any shadows. The lack of shadows gives the resultant image a somewhat flat quality, rarely three-dimensional. This type of lighting provides clean and intense colors, allows for a long shooting distance, and in portraits, causes wrinkles to disappear and makes skin look smoother. Front lighting enhances the subject's colors without causing shadows that make the subject's shape more complex, which is why this type of lighting is ideal for certain color shots and whenever shadows are not wanted in the picture.

With the flash off camera: Moving the light source off-camera by positioning the flash unit relatively high, either in your hand or with a bracket, provides front light directed from above. This lighting creates small shadows that slightly emphasize the subject's shape and outline. Thus, for rendering shape and depth, high front light is more suitable than front lighting positioned lower.

Front light with diffusers: When front light is directional and not diffused, it may produce unflattering dark shadows around the subject's eyes and below the nose. But, when sufficiently diffused, this light is particularly convenient whenever there is no time or reason for special illumination, and it can provide far-reaching lighting without a significant loss of brightness. This type of light is ideal for all kinds of snapshots, for weddings, family events, and parties, for running pets and playing children. It is the simplest method of achieving surprisingly uniform lighting on several subjects at various distances, by photographing from a greater distance with a telephoto lens.

Side Light at a 45 Degree Angle

This light is often used for portraits and will be described in detail in conjunction with this field of photography. It can be set up easily for indoor photographs. An indirect or diffused light source, which reduces contrast, is usually preferable to direct light.

Side Light at a 90 Degree Angle

This extreme, but mood-enhancing light is produced when the flash unit is at an angle of 90 degrees, relative to the camera - that is, the subject is lighted directly from the side. The lower the position of the flash, the easier it is to simulate the beautiful light that occurs in early morning or late evening. Side-lighting is always dramatic and produces extreme contrast, which generally needs to be reduced, especially in color photography. Side-lighting strongly emphasizes the three-dimensional appearance of any surface because it forms highlights and shadows that accentuate every irregularity. For portraits, this type of light must be used very carefully, however, when used correctly, it is the light of experts.

Backlight

If the flash unit casts light from behind the subject toward the camera lens, the result is backlight. Backlight is less intense when it is bounced from the ceiling, slightly offset behind the subject. This is certainly the most mood-enhancing type of lighting and can add drama to a portrait, but it also produces the greatest contrast and may make optimum illumination quite difficult.

Backlight produces bright highlights and large dark shadows that are cast in the direction of the camera. This intensifies the impression of spatial depth and can emphasize surface textures, at certain angles.

For a romantic effect: At its extreme, backlight creates a silhouette effect, producing dramatic images that come alive strictly because of their outline. However, backlighting can also be used for subjects such as portraits and flowers, to produce delicate light outlines or halos that convey a romantic flair. If you use a soft-focus attachment on the camera lens, backlight literally frames the subject with radiant light, arousing romantic or celestial feelings in any viewer. However, the lighting contrast and subject contrast must not be too extreme. Ideally, the illumination of the halo should exceed the correct basic exposure by no more than one f/stop. Only tiny highlights, such as reflections on hair, should be brighter. Backlight is probably the only kind of lighting that allows this degree of mood manipulation by adjusting the exposure. Achieving correct exposure with backlight can be surprisingly simple when you use automatic fill flash or cordless TTL metering.

Reflected Light as Fill Light

The most important reflected light for the photographer is the light used for reducing contrast, or indirect light created by a lighting system. This can easily be produced by attaching a reflector to the flash unit. This lighting is ideal for outdoor photos and snapshots and can even be used for simple portrait lighting. Using a reflector reduces the effect of front light. However, because the reflector surface is relatively small, this type of fill light is limited to subjects that are close to the camera.

Softening light with bounce flash: Other forms of supplemental lighting are more effective for off-camera flash pictures, especially portraits or still life photos taken in a home studio. Obviously, white ceilings and walls represent the least complicated softening option. However, this is ideal only when the light is sufficient for acceptable basic lighting throughout the room, for instance when photographing a group of people.

Using panels: White "foam-core" panels, available at art supply stores, or professional reflector panels such as those supplied by Domke offer a highly effective solution. They are ideal reflectors because they give you complete control over the light path.

The path to the reflecting surface (thus the size of this surface), as well as the brightening effect, may be modified directly by the photographer by changing the distance. It is amazing how shadow rendition is improved by such a simple reduction of contrast.

This technique is advantageous for still lifes and some close-ups, especially when additional ambient light is not available. A

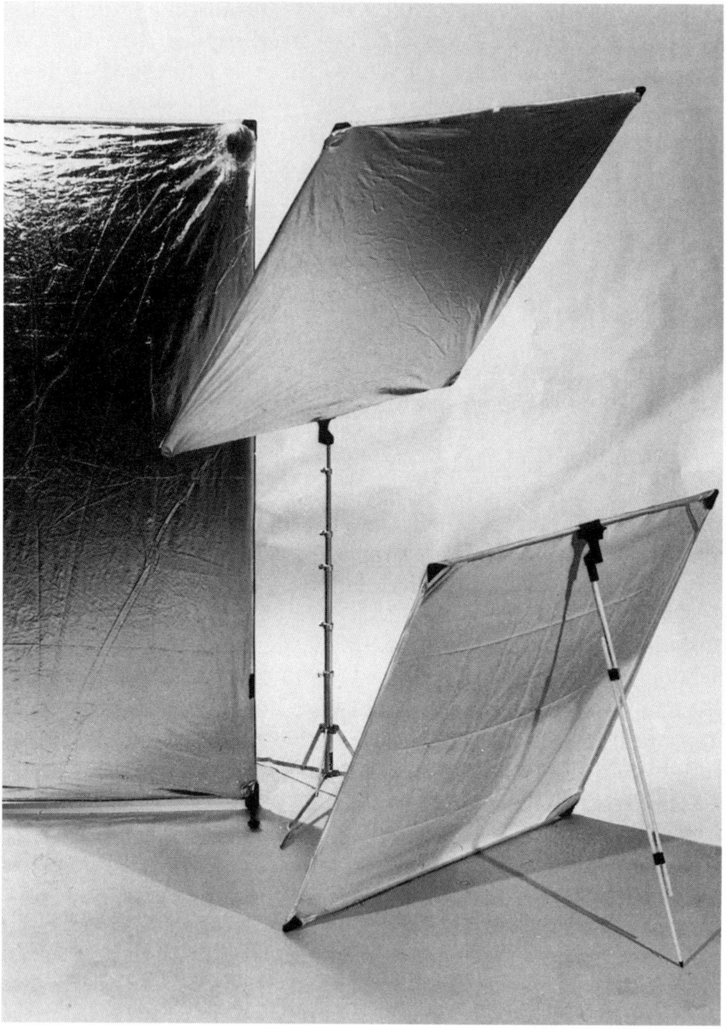

Reflector panels, such as these Domke LiteFRAMES, in gold, silver, and white can be used to soften light and reduce deep shadows.

single flash unit can provide enough illumination, especially when a portion of the flash is directed at the reflector, for example, via a mirror.

Professional reflector panels include mounting accessories. To hold homemade reflector panels in place, you can use a large paint bucket or can filled with plaster or cement, with a tripod screw embedded at the top to attach a ball-and-socket joint. If you have a light stand, adapters to hold reflector panels are available.

Firing into an umbrella: There are other convenient and more compact ways of using light to brighten a subject. Many suppliers offer a variety of studio umbrella reflectors with white, silver or gold linings. The only accessory needed is a mounting bracket to attach the umbrella and flash unit to the light stand. The flash unit is aimed at the curved underside of the umbrella, which diffuses the light and reflects it back to the subject. Umbrella light is relatively soft and you can further soften it to some extent by attaching a wide-angle diffuser to the flash unit or by moving the flash farther from the umbrella. (Conversely, moving the flash unit closer to the umbrella makes the light harsher.)

Color considerations diffusers or reflectors: When choosing diffusers and surfaces for reflected fill light, you must consider that the color of the reflector will affect the color of the reflected light. This can be an advantage, for example, using a gold-colored reflector for portraits will create warm-colored highlights that resemble evening light. This gold color is also used for special effects in fashion and glamour photography. By comparison, the light reflected by silver reflectors is the same color as the light source and often appears "cold" or "cool."

When choosing reflector surfaces and materials, you must check them for unexpected color casts. This is especially important when using walls and ceilings for bounce light. Of course, surfaces that are obviously colored are not suitable for color photography with bounce lighting, but even surfaces that appear to be white may cause a color cast.

Connections for off-camera flash: A flash unit used with an umbrella can be connected to the camera via a simple extension sync cord; cordlessly with a photocell, a Mecalux 11, or a Mecamat; via a TTL Multiblitz connector cable; or with the slave adapter for cordless TTL flash metering. Note that if the flash is controlled by a photocell, the photocell must face toward the subject, not toward the umbrella. If this is not possible and the photocell can only be aimed at the umbrella, you must use a correction factor and open the camera lens wider than the f/stop indicated by the flash unit. The correction will usually be in the range of 1 or 2 stops, but must be determined by tests.

If you use several flash units together, you must be careful to prevent the light from one flash unit from influencing the photocell on another flash. You can block the direct light from the other flash by using off-camera techniques or by using dark cardboard gobos.

Metering: When using flash for fill, the exact amount of light is not too critical as long as it is kept at least one f/stop below the level of the existing ambient illumination. However, exposures made completely with flash require an accurate division of the light from each flash unit. Such precise control of the light can be obtained by using the Mecamat, TTL metering with the Multiconnector, or cordless TTL metering with a Mecablitz 40 MZ 2.

Diffused Light

There are three types of diffuse light. There is reflected light, as just described, reflected by a diffuser near the subject. There is diffuse light created by passing the light through a translucent diffusing screen. The result is relatively low-contrast lighting with only faint shadows, making this technique ideal for showing subtle nuances of color. This type of lighting is used for portraits, fashion photography, and advertising photography. And there is the diffuse light found outdoors in bright shaded areas, known as open shade.

Filtered Light

Filtered light is light that has passed through translucent material (a scrim) such as fabric. If the material is pure white, the light will remain white, but if it is colored, naturally the transmitted light will also be colored. (An example is the light under a colored sun umbrella.)

Pure white studio umbrellas can be used for controlled light filtering. By projecting the flash through them, they produce highly diffused light. A light loss of 2 to 3 f/stops is typical when the lighting is filtered through an umbrella. This is particularly important to remember in telecomputer control mode, as the light loss may be too much to allow correct exposure. To overcome this, the photographer must use powerful flash units, and of course, Metz handle-mount flash units can provide this level of power.

Just as when indirect flash is used with a reflector, flash projected through an umbrella or scrim must be metered with the flash unit's photocell facing the subject, and it must not be blocked by the umbrella or diffuser.

Large-Area Light Sources

Large-area light sources often used in professional photography include soft boxes. They produce soft, sometimes even amazingly low-contrast light, with delicate shadows, rarely with distinct contours. This type of lighting is very suitable for basic illumination. Only a light tent would be considered a more powerful large-area light and offer completely shadow-free illumination.

Soft boxes: A number of firms including Photoflex, Sailwind, Larsen and Westcott offer soft boxes. The front diffuser screen consists of white translucent material. The outer fabric shell has a silver (or gold) coating on the inside and is black on the outside. The silver coating inside the shell allows the light to exit only through the front of the soft box. On some soft boxes the flash unit mounts inside, by means of a flash unit holder, and on others the flash mounts on the back of the softbox.

Soft boxes use light efficiently, with little light loss, and diffuse it very softly. On the models in which the flash in enclosed within the softbox, the flash can be fired via a photocell or a Mecalux 11; however, the photocell must be placed outside the box and connected with a cable so that it can be pointed directly at another flash.

In spite of their size, soft boxes are ideal for portrait photography, which is why smaller studios may find this type of unit very useful.

On-camera flash modifiers: For on-camera flash, umbrellas and similar accessories are usually too large and bulky, but a number of small units are available to produce a similar effect. One of the

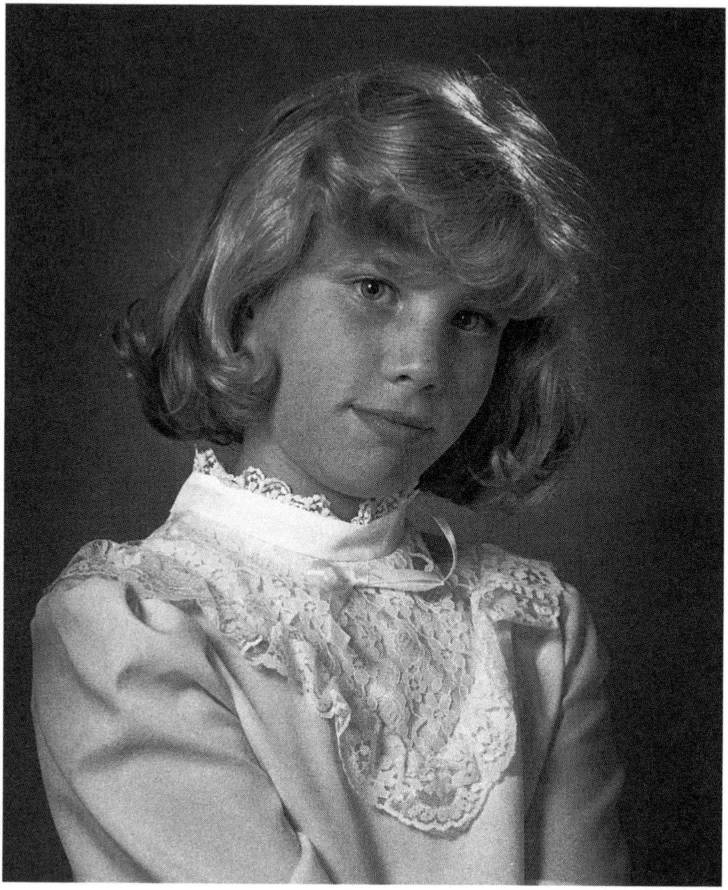

Two flash units and a reflector panel created the soft, pleasing light in this portrait. Photo: Peter K. Burian

authors, Bob Shell, uses a Photoflex Inflatable XTC miniature softbox almost all of the time for direct fill flash. This unit is exceptionally nice because it collapses to a tiny size for storage and transport, and is simply inflated like a balloon prior to use and attached to the flash with Velcro™ tabs. The Lumiquest company also makes a line of very nice diffusers which bounce the light to the subject. Perhaps the best of these is the Big Bounce. Folded for storage it is approximately the size of a sheet of letter-size paper, and it comes with an auxiliary diffuser shade, ensuring additional diffusion of the light from a completely enclosed flash reflector. The Big Bounce may be used successfully for portraits and close-ups, and can serve as a portable small soft box. However, if space is available, a full-sized soft box is unbeatable.

Composition of Lighting

Backgrounds with deep shadows are almost always acceptable in outdoor photographs, but indoors they appear out of place except in large spaces such as auditoriums or houses of worship. This demonstrates that although correct exposure is important (and seems to satisfy most photographers), correct illumination is even more important. Proper illumination not only produces correct exposure, it is the photographer's first and most important creative tool.

It is good practice to set up lighting in two stages. First is the ambient basic light, either existing light or flash, which determines the picture's overall mood. Second is fill light and/or effect light from the flash, which is used to direct the viewer's eyes to the important feature in the picture.

The secondary light sources used for fill light or effect light rarely overpower the basic lighting, so usually the exposure needs no adjustment or only a minimal adjustment. In some cases, however, the combination of the basic light plus the fill light in highlight areas may be excessive, and this will require an exposure correction.

Correct Fill Light

Photographers who utilize the existing ambient light and mood only need to determine the amount of fill flash. If general scenes or portraits are the subject, a typical arrangement would be setting the fill flash 1 f/stop less than the ambient light level. With slide film, a brightness difference of 1-1/2 to 2 stops difference may be preferable.

Lighting Effects Created by Shadows

There are other lighting effects rarely used by photographers. We all are familiar with the image used in mystery movies, where we see the shadow of a hand aiming a pistol at the victim. Because shadows are the negative aspect of light, using shadows for effect can be considered a light effect. Such shadow effects can be applied to the background as well as to the main subject. One example would be the effect caused by light shining through a venetian blind, covering the background with an effective shadow pattern of stripes.

Effective Shadows with Cookies

The term "cookie" is motion picture industry slang for a light modifier properly known as a Cuculoris, presumably named after the inventor. Cookies are masks made of opaque material such as wood, plastic, paper, metal foil or fiberglass. Simple patterns are cut out of them, for example, window frames, grids to resemble light cast into a jail cell through the bars, or strips that create the "venetian blind" effect. However, even a simple circle, an irregular hole pattern, or any shape that provides a useful or mood-conveying silhouette can be used as a cookie.

Adding background moods and effects: Cookies used in still photography are usually about the size of a piece of writing paper, but can be considerably larger, and are clamped to light stands and placed between the background and the hard, direct light from a flash unit. By using cookies, even the largest wall or any plain, featureless background can be given an intended mood and brought to life. Cookies are sold ready-made by Matthews (supplier to the Hollywood cinema industry), and thin sheets of soft, black aluminum (really heavy-gauge foil), designed to be cut into custom cookies, are available from several photo suppliers.

Experiment for best results: To acquire expertise in the use of light and shadow, the much-cited American photographer and author Andreas Feininger suggests that photographers should experiment with a practice subject such as a large white cube or a plaster copy of a famous statue such as the Venus de Milo, or even use a patient live model. To develop your skill at placing light and "playing with light," an excellent prop for experimentation is one of the inexpensive Styrofoam heads sold for storing wigs. With any of these, you can make a lighting book with sketches of different lighting arrangements and the resulting images. This makes an excellent reference tool. (This is especially easy to do using a Polaroid camera.)

Deep Subjects

Since the light released by the flash decreases in proportion to the square of the distance, a distinct distance between the foreground and the background frequently becomes a "black hole."

Flash exposures with slow shutter speeds: The "black hole" situation occurs typically in larger, poorly-illuminated rooms. If there is noticeable ambient light and the subjects are not moving, this situation can be handled by using a slower shutter speed. Unlike the choice of aperture, which affects the flash-exposed foreground, the choice of shutter speed affects only the ambient light (and therefore, the background) exposure.

For almost all cameras: By using manual exposure adjustment on the camera, shutter speeds which are slower than the typical flash synchronization speed may be selected for use with flash (even with TTL flash mode).

For cameras offering slow synchronization with TTL: When an aperture appropriate for the desired depth of field has been preselected, this flash mode will automatically adjust the background brightness in accordance with the exposure time, in aperture priority and programmed autoflash. Don't forget to use a tripod and a self-timer or cable release to prevent camera movement. Moving subjects will be blurred with low ambient light and slow shutter speeds. If this is desirable, it is better to use a slow shutter speed with automatic aperture adjustment.

Multiple Flash Lighting of Spatially Deep Subjects

In order to lighten the background several flash units in addition to the camera-mounted flash can be fired, either with TTL cords, Metz remote wireless TTL flash control mode, or with "slaves." With cameras offering TTL auto fill flash, note that this mode responds to the ambient light metered before the flash is fired, additional flash units may over-lighten the background. Therefore, a fully manual flash exposure determined by using a hand-held flash meter is often recommended.

Controlling Background Brightness

It is not always desirable that the background and the foreground have the same brightness level resulting from fill flash. In order to "set-off" the main subject against the background, it may be advantageous to make the background darker or lighter. Many recent cameras offer this option using manual exposure adjustment in combination with TTL autoflash. If your camera offers this with the appropriate SCA adapter follow this procedure:

1. The Metz flash must be set on "TTL".
2. Using manual "M" camera exposure mode, first set the aperture appropriate for a shutter speed between 1/60 second and 1/250 second Meter the main subject by using either spot or center-weighted metering and then adjust the exposure as if shooting without flash.
3. The aperture determined in this manner may be closed down approximately 2 to 3 stops to make the background distinctly darker or opened up approximately 2 to 3 stops to make the background distinctly lighter.

After some trial and error, it should be possible to achieve the desired effect on the first try. (By increasing the ISO film speed setting, cameras with conventional TTL autoflash are effectively set for a minus correction which affects only the flash. *Caution:* Be careful not to base the ambient exposure on this "adjusted" ISO speed.

Additional adjustment of background and foreground brightness: By using opposing exposure compensations on the camera versus the flash, the brightness values of the foreground and the background may be manipulated or brought closer to each other. However, in order to arrive at reliable results a few test exposures should be made.

Auxiliary Flash for Background Illumination

Using an auxiliary flash unit can solve the problem of significant brightness differences in a room and can overcome a dark background. If the room permits, set up the auxiliary flash high behind you, or to one side, and bounce the light off a white wall or ceiling. The larger the lighted area on the ceiling or wall, the better the lighting will be. Because bounce light is no longer a point source, the room can be lighted with surprising uniformity.

For example, to photograph a party taking place in a large room, set up a second handle-mount flash unit at the other end of the room, hidden from view, to provide bounce lighting. Set both flash units to computerized aperture mode and aim the sensor to measure the light reflected by the subject. The flashes are then fired via a photocell or a Mecalux photocell. When using this technique, be careful not to fire flashes in too rapid a succession, because the auxiliary flash units need sufficient time to recycle.

This technique is useful for surprisingly uniform illumination of average-size to very large rooms where fashion shows, gallery openings, weddings, and other such events may take place. In these situations the basic light of the auxiliary flash units can also be used as fill light. To do this, set the computerized aperture one f/stop smaller than the aperture setting of the main flash on the camera. The light quality can be improved further by using a diffuser on the main flash to soften the light.

Creative Use of Fill Flash

Electronic flash is the photographer's private sun giving rise to novel views and perspectives. It is the most versatile type of light that is always at the photographer's disposal. A photographer may aim it directly or bounce it, diffuse it or create shadows, filter or polarize it. While ambient light imparts a situation or subject with a mood, an additional small dose of flash can enhance the picture and clearly establish this mood. Flash light can be used to amplify or negate an existing light situation. This is true for brightness, colors, contrast, light direction and shadow formation.

As fill light, flash is used as an auxiliary light source in addition to available light and is totally subordinate to the prevailing mood in a photograph picture. Even the most difficult lighting conditions which occur at dusk or at night may be improved with fill flash.

Also, no difference is made among fill flash, filled-in extended exposure or night exposure with fill flash. The proportion of flash light is determined based on individual problems and subjects and must be tested frequently by using different values.

Fill flash light may:

1. Act as an additional light source to supplement existing light.
2. Lighten deep shadows.
3. Eliminate the blue tinge caused by overcast skies or shade.
4. Eliminate or reduce the yellow-orange tinge of sunrise or sunset.
5. Eliminate color reflections; e.g. from colored umbrellas or awnings.
6. Give portraits a more youthful look
7. Darken a low-contrast light background.
8. Allow smaller apertures for better depth of field and color.
9. Produce more artistic extended-exposure images and night exposures.
10. Add colored accents with filters.

The Question of Contrast

Contrast is generally expressed in three levels: normal, high and low. The concept of "normal contrast" is used when the highlights and shadows in the subject are within the range of the photographic medium and can be reproduced in detail. A high contrast photograph has a compressed tonal range with fewer shades of gray between pure black and pure white. The terms crisp, snappy or harsh are sometimes used to describe high contrast images. Low contrast images have an expanded tonal range, but may look flat, dull or "muddy" because both pure white and pure black cannot be reproduced.

Way back in 1939, Andreas Feininger, the American photographer and author, wrote "Backlighting is darkness flooded by light." He raved about this form of light, contours adorned by halos and deep shadows which can be made lighter to enhance contrast. Unfortunately, backlighting can be difficult to reproduce to show its true impact and strong light/dark contrasts.

The most beautiful backlighting exists early in the morning or late in the afternoon when the light just grazes a subject but is

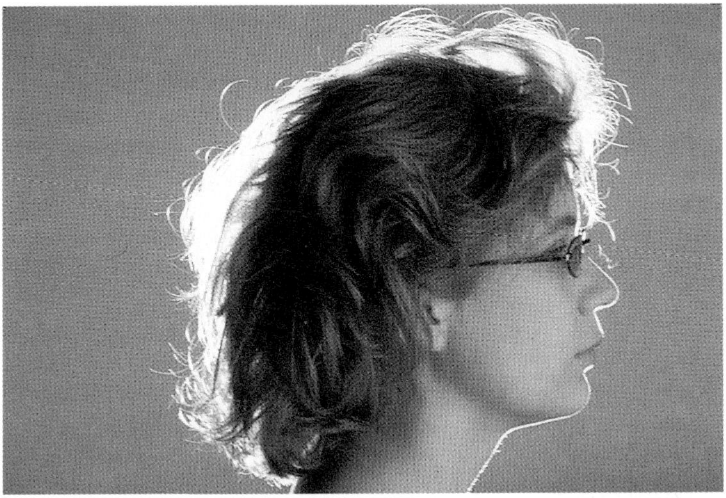

Strong backlighting is created by positioning a flash unit behind the subject and setting it to output two to three stops more light than the aperture set on the lens.

still quite intense. In these situations, colors may be intensified by fill flash. Also the richness of detail in the low-key areas and therefore, the overall mood of the picture may be enhanced.

Parameters applicable to normal backlighting may also be used for filling in silhouettes that occur in front of a large living room window backlit by sunshine. This situation requires that the exposure be adjusted for the shadows because the resultant bright overexposed background is always unpleasant. The simplest way to succeed in this situation is to expose for the high-key areas and use fill flash.

Contrast compensation: The flash's contrast-enhancing effect must not be forgotten. The photographer may play "sun" with his electronic flash light when, on dreary days, low-contrast subjects appear to have no color at all or when the sky or background should look darker and more dramatic. Fill flash only imparts every detail of the subject within shooting distance with more light and hence more luminance. Image contrast is increased slightly. If the exposure adjustment is based on lightest areas of

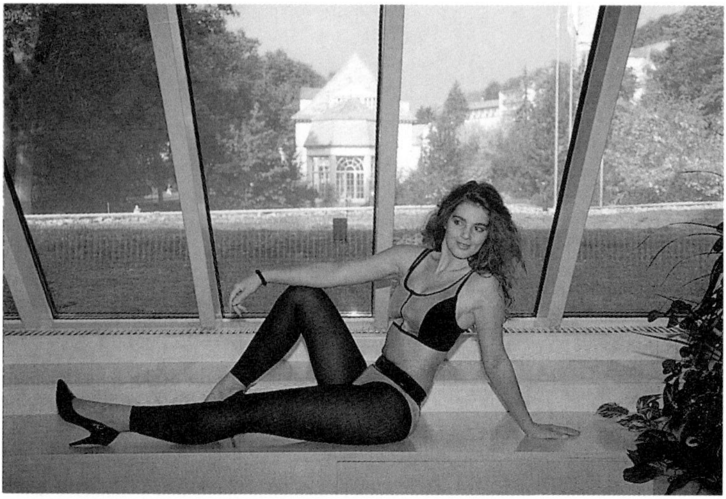

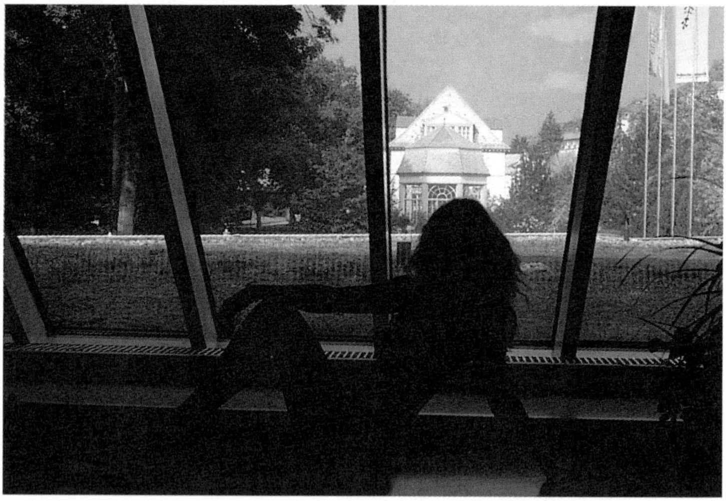

Without fill flash, the model in the bottom picture appears as a silhouette in the foreground.

the subject, the background will appear darker. A maximum contrast increase requires the same aperture adjustment on the flash unit and on the camera lens. In order to prevent overexposure, each unit is adjusted to double the ISO speed or to a -1 EV correction. In this case ambient light (like flash light) provides 50% of the total illumination. The exposure will be correct only in areas covered by both types of light. Wherever only one light source is active, an underexposure of 1 f/stop (i.e., darkening) will be noticed.

Fill Flash with High-Speed Films

High-speed film materials can produce pictures with fill characteristics at extremely great shooting distances which are hardly imaginable by amateur, or even some professional photographers.

Extending shooting distances: The film industry provides the photographer with super high-speed ISO 1000 films. With the 85mm reflector setting of the Mecablitz 40 MZ 2, a metric guide number of 150 is realized with ISO 1000 film. But that is not all. This high-speed film material may be pushed to 3200 and the same flash unit then has a metric guide number of 250. Even a low-power zoom unit permits a sufficient shooting distance, using f/8 and 1000 speed film up to 60 feet (20 m) and at 3200 up to even 90 feet (30 m). If the light from the flash is used only for fill flash, it therefore requires less (flash) light than is required by the adjusted time/aperture combination, thus, the reach is increased by 50%. Depending on the desired fill-light level, a difference of 2 f/stops may even double the distance at which a fill flash effect is evident. Using a fast, fixed focal length lens at f/2, this means a metric guide number of 150 divided by f/2 produces a flash exposure at a shooting distance of 225 feet (75 m), which can be extended to at least 360 feet (120 m) without additional units.

Even though the aperture of a Minolta xi in automatic programmed mode may be opened only to f/2.8, the shooting distance reaches up to 159 feet (53 m) and, in fully automatic mode, up to approximately 300 feet (100 m)! However, it must be considered that the working range of most camera flash metering systems reaches its limit at ISO 1000. Those, who question the practical applicability of such high guide numbers, have probably not yet worked with high and super-high film speeds. And those, who were not satisfied with high-speed imaging because the paper prints were grainy and muddy looking, may improve future pictures with a touch of flash.

Those, who have been shaking their heads because someone in the upper rows of a stadium takes a flash picture of the playing field or the stage, have to look more carefully now and note whether that someone is taking a fill flash picture of rock singer Tina Turner from a distance of well over 300 feet (100 m). Thanks to fill flash and high-speed films the illumination of large spaces has become a possibility. The advantage of this technology is that a whole building, inside and out, may be converted into pictures expressing beautiful moods requiring only a touch of flash light without very long exposure times.

Fill Flash for Deep Shadows

Even more than backlit subjects, deep shadows present a typical situation for fill flash. At noon, deep shadows may unfavorably model a face; this effect may be offset with large-surface reflectors or a touch of fill flash. Properly metered flash used as auxiliary or fill light in sunshine, provides harmonious overall illumination, ensures clear colors and enhances the mood of a picture. Plus, the catchlight in the subject's eyes always adds life to the picture.

Using reflectors with fill flash: The risk of distinct, dark shadows can be reduced by fill flash exposure using the largest-available reflector. Soft light will not produce such deep shadows. Reflectors are available for handle-mount units and now Metz SCA 3000 compact flash units. Or Lumiquest reflectors may be conveniently attached to the flash head.

Eliminating Color Tinges

Color enhancement is equally important. For example, a blue cast commonly found if the subject is in shade, may be eliminated easily with fill flash. Rather than placing a large group of people, for example a wedding party, in bright sunlight and unnecessarily increasing the contrast caused by white and black clothing, people should be photographed in the shade. However, the background must not be illuminated or the exposure must be adjusted appropriately. A small portion of additional light makes the white, as well as all the other colors, more brilliant and eliminates the strong blue tinge in the shade. The result is harmoniously illuminated pictures.

Wherever flash light reaches, color is reflected by areas of portraits or snapshots taken in the shade. It is a matter of taste whether the filled in area should be clearly obvious to the viewer or reduced to a minimum. If the camera is capable of influencing the flash intensity by means of an automatic minus-correction, this option should be used for precise control of the amount of fill flash.

Eliminating other types of color tinges: There are many types of color casts. For example, a bright sunset produces yellow or red tinges. This too, may be trimmed to a perfectly neutral color within the flash shooting distance. The photographer must evaluate each new situation individually; experience has shown, however, that a color cast should not necessarily be interpreted as undesirable.

Also, unpleasant color reflections under a colored sun umbrella (e.g., at a market stand, at the beach or in the garden) may be eliminated and a possible color tinge removed by a small amount of fill flash.

Fill Flash at a Sunset

We all have seen the magnificent brochures of fantastic hotels where a sunset may be admired from a terrace or even one's room. In the future, such pictures may be taken without problems by using fill flash. The exposure may even be adapted to the sun so that the fiery sun ball will appear as colorful and brilliant as possible. Fill flash can be used to impart people sitting in the foreground with enough color, shadows and definition. Models need no longer be just silhouettes.

Fill Flash to Flatter a Portrait Subject

Frontal flash mounted directly on the camera suppresses wrinkles and produces clearly improved skin color. Those thinking of golden brown sun-basked skin, however, should not depend too much on their cameras. This type of light still contains a large portion of UV light which tends to emphasize skin impurities and small blood vessels. A filter attached in front of the reflector, a Skylight 3 or a warm-color amber filter, helps achieve ideal skin tones. Kodak offers these filters in the form of plastic sheeting which may be cut to fit a flash unit's reflector. One of the authors, Bob Shell, is noted for his glamour photography and

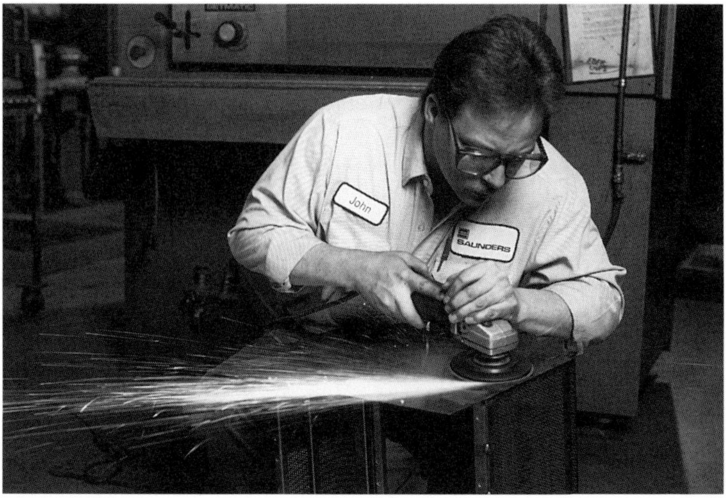

Flash was used to expose the subject in this enviromental portrait, but a slow shutter speed produced the ambient light exposure in the background, as well as the dramatic display of sparks.
Photo: Mike McWilliams

always fits a piece of Rosco filter gel over his flash head for fill flash. The color preferred has the odd name of Bastard Amber, and comes in lighter and darker versions. Every portrait will appear more youthful when illuminated in this manner and, if possible, modeled softly.

Slow Shutter Speeds with Fill Flash

Technically, there is no difference between fill flash with the higher range of sync speeds and fill flash exposures made with slow shutter speeds. In this case, the camera determines the correct exposure. Therefore, it is not important whether it is 1/30 second, 3 seconds, or 30 seconds. The only concern is that picture may be blurred if the camera-determined ambient exposure is too long. In all the examples listed here, flash lighting represents a small but carefully determined added amount of light.

When using slow shutter speeds with fill flash, the specific exposure technique is determined by your camera. You can use slower shutter speeds only when the background is darker. This is desirable so the photograph will retain the mood of a location, or the mood at night. The existing ambient light determines the mood of the picture, and the correct amount of fill flash is used, to provide motion-stopping light on the subject in the foreground.

In practical applications, especially when you want to show subtle differences using color slide film, it makes sense to place the exposure emphasis on the darkest areas. This way, the mood is maintained and the brightening effect on the overall picture is not conspicuous. In addition, when very small areas in the foreground will be filled in with flash, you should make a minus correction for the total exposure to reduce the intensity of the fill flash.

Making a test exposure: To determine exactly how much light is lost, you can fire a test flash. Switch the flash unit to automatic mode (A-mode) and fire the flash without using the secondary reflector. If the flash "OK" indicator on the flash does not light up following the test flash, open the lens one f/stop and repeat the test. (Naturally, you must keep the camera and flash unit in the same position for the test flash and the "real" exposure.)

In cordless mode: This technique may also be used in cordless mode and integrated with corrected TTL metering, even for extended exposures. This can be done with certain Maxxum/Dynax xi cameras, and with all other cameras by using two Metz 40 MZ 2 flash units. This technique requires allowing the flash unit to recycle completely before each photograph. (Remember that the flash readiness indicator will light at only 70% of full charge.) The blinking indicator in the viewfinder and the "OK" signal on the Mecablitz verify that flash output was adequate for a correct exposure.

For night photography: Slow shutter speed flash exposures prevent the background in night exposures from becoming pitch black, as it would when using faster shutter speeds. This way the picture retains the original mood found by the photographer and the effect is always more natural than in flash-only pictures. In addition, the maximum shooting range is doubled in fill flash mode. Blurring the picture is not a concern because the short flash duration creates a sharp image of the main subject. If you also want the background to be sharp and blur-free, however, using a tripod is advisable.

Creative Solutions with Flash

Flash is also recommended for purely creative solutions. For example, two or three pictures may be taken of severely backlit subjects "in a flash" while changing the subject itself but not the ambient mood. A silhouette may first be measured with emphasis on high-key areas, then (optionally fully automatically) in fill flash mode and sometimes even flash-only mode, and then with a dark background. The technique used with individual fill flash is determined by the camera and the flash unit. For example, Leica R7 and Minolta Maxxum/Dynax cameras require an automatic exposure adjustment; Canon EOS and Nikon cameras use more sensible automatic balanced fill flash in aperture priority. The latter is considered more sensible because the variable, stepless shutter speed range comprises a greater range than one series of lens apertures. Also shutter priority offers an astonishingly simple way to add light when cameras without TTL flash metering option are used. The end of this chapter includes an easy to follow step-by-step description for specific cameras and flash units.

For cameras without dedicated systems: Following are some basic principles applying to cameras which do not allow the use of automatic SCA Adapter control. An aperture greater than the highest sync speed is selected on the camera (A, in aperture priority after preselecting the aperture). In "telecomputer" flash operation mode without TTL metering, an aperture is determined on the flash unit. Some cameras require a standard SCA 301 foot to prevent them from switching automatically to X-speed. Depending on the shooting distance, the aperture to be set on the flash unit should normally be 2 f/stops wider than the lens aperture. If f/8 has been preselected on the lens, the flash is normally set to 4. The aperture opening adjusted on the flash unit must at all times be wider than that on the lens. This applies to a shooting distance of up to approximately 12 feet (4 m) at which sufficient light is reflected by the subject. Experience has shown that greater distances require a difference of 3 f/stops.

A great number of subjects reflect significant diffuse light which does not return to the camera (outdoors or large halls). The flash unit works harder because it is "looking for" a certain amount of reflected light. Unfortunately, the photographer has no control over this condition; in isolated cases he may use a Mecamat for precise control. Therefore, a photographer adjusts 3 f/stops faster, even though later added lighting is to be only 2 additional f/stops (as a result of extended flash duration).

This technique of using a difference of 2 f/stops and a touch of flash to lighten a subject may be applied to all areas of a subject. In this case it is seriously recommended that the value and difference between normal and auxiliary flash be tested to determine personal exposure preferences. Those, who always work with high-key metering, end up with a somewhat greater amount of flash exposure and hence lighter pictures than those who take exposures based on the weighted grey value.

Adding Color Accents

Adding color accents is common in motion picture and video production, especially in music videos. Intense colors and colored lights are often used to create a variety of moods. "Lifestyle" magazines like to use similar visual tricks, and even respected newspapers sometimes print flash pictures with highly accented colors.

Since viewers accept these color-enhanced pictures, why not experiment with wild colors once in a while and accent a series of pictures with colored flash? You can use color accents with all fill flash and daylight flash techniques to make your photos more dramatic.

In theory, using colored flash lighting is easy; in reality, it is surprisingly difficult. You should begin with a good command of daylight photography using flash and fill flash, and have a powerful flash unit with a guide number of at least 120 for feet, 35 for meters.

Examples of the diverse effects you can create with colored filters are:

1. Colored flash in the foreground.
2. Blue night shots with color correct foreground.
3. Colored background and corrected foreground.
4. Colored background with unchanged foreground.

Sources for color effect "filters": There are many sources for colored filters. Metz offers special filter kits for both the new models

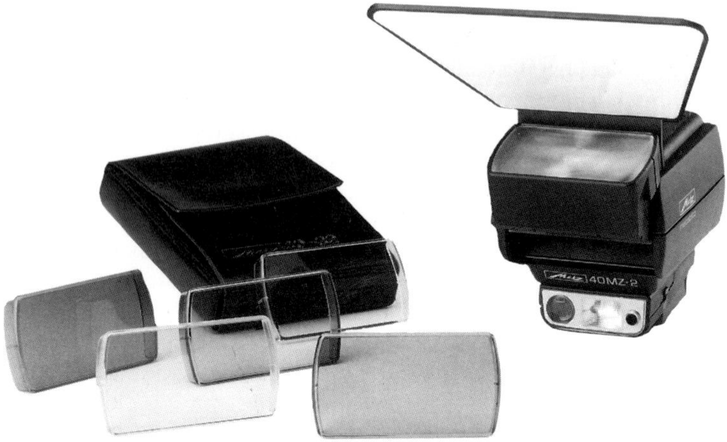

The Mecablitz 40 MZ 2 is shown here with a Metz bounce diffuser. Light-reducing filters balance the illumination when several flash units are combined. The color filters are mainly used for creative lighting effects.

of compact flash units and the handle-mount units; these filters are available in red, green, yellow and blue. Color filters used in black-and-white photography can also be used; a strong blue filter is particularly effective. Other sources for filters include colored plastic gels from Cokin, Lee, Rosco, and other suppliers; colored acetate sheet material used in graphic arts; colored plastic report binder covers and other colored materials found in art supply stores; colored sheet material used in overhead projectors; and even colored cellophane and plastic product wrappers. These "homemade" filters can be attached in front of the flash with Velcro tape (available by the yard from many suppliers) or simply with a piece of adhesive tape, if no appropriate filter holder is available. With all colored filters, and particularly with home-made filters, a series of test exposures is needed to see the exact effect.

For most photography, when sharp pictures are required, you should not use the inexpensive, optically imperfect materials mentioned above on the camera lens, only on the flash unit. However, for mood photos and other pictures in which sharpness is not critical, even the inexpensive materials can be used on the lens, attached with tape or rubber bands.

Colored flash in the foreground: To add color to just the foreground, mount a color filter in front of the flash reflector. When you take the picture, everything within the effective range of the flash will acquire a color cast, strongest close to the flash unit and becoming weaker farther away. This can also be used with fill flash, in which case the color cast shows in the shadow regions and wherever flash illumination is predominant. However, practical tests have shown that the effect will be stronger and more noticeable if no fill flash is used and the film sensitivity is adjusted on the camera to twice or four times its actual ISO value. This makes the flash-exposed background distinctly darker and more dramatic. The aperture required for proper exposure at the actual ISO speed should be set on the flash unit; an EV adjustment of -1 is always recommended, considering the low reflection in outdoor exposures.

Blue night shots and corrected foreground: You can add extraordinary color casts reminiscent of special-effect cinema lighting relatively easily. A particularly effective combination is using Tungsten-type film in daylight situations, together with an orange or yellow filter on the flash unit. Within the effective range of the flash, the warm-colored filter provides light that is approximately like tungsten light in color, so within this range the colors are normal or nearly normal. But the rest of the image, which was not illuminated by the flash, turns a silvery blue-grey color. This effect creates intense colors in pictures taken at dusk or at night. This technique will produce even more dramatic pictures when the exposure meter is adjusted to twice the normal ISO value, or a minus correction is made.

Colored background with corrected foreground: This is a straightforward effect that requires at least two flash units. Use one to light the foreground normally, with white light, and put a colored filter on the other unit(s) used to illuminate the background. For example, making fashion shots at a swimming pool and intensifying the blue color of the water: Use blue filters on the background lighting and aim it to illuminate the pool but not the model and foreground. The additional flash unit(s) can be triggered with extension sync cords, IR remote control, or slave units.

Colored background with normal foreground: This is a more complicated effect. You can color the background but leave the foreground unchanged by placing a colored filter on the camera lens and attaching a second filter, complementary in color, to the flash unit. The area correctly exposed by the flash will appear normal in color while the background, illuminated by ambient light, will show an increasing color cast (the color of the filter on the lens).

With all these techniques, use care not to exceed the range of the flash, and remember that this will be decreased because of the light absorbed by the filters, both on the camera lens and on the flash unit itself.

Eliminating Reciprocity Failure with Flash

When color films are used for long exposures, even with the correct light source, most of them suffer from reciprocity failure, which produces an unpleasant color cast, often green or blue. Reciprocity failure (technically known as the Schwarzschild Effect) occurs because the individual emulsion layers in the film, which react identically at normal exposure times, react dissimilarly during very long exposures. Some color films show reciprocity failure even at 1/15 second, and it occurs in most color films when a shutter speed longer than 1 second is used. (This color shift should not be confused with the color shifts caused by using light sources that are not properly balanced for the film being used, for example using incandescent bulbs with Daylight-type film, or using fluorescent lamps, which do not match either Daylight-type or Tungsten-type color films.)

The color shifts caused by reciprocity failure can be "flashed away" by using electronic flash, which is balanced for daylight-type films (its color characteristics are very similar to natural daylight). Doing this requires no more flash than the usual fill flash exposure. Within the flash unit's effective range, its light will eliminate the color cast or at least reduce it to an acceptable level.

Freezing the Action

In the past the shutter speed range of most cameras included 1/1000 second as the fastest exposure time for non-blurred representation of fast-action. With high speeds up to 1/4000 second and 1/8000 second offered by modern cameras, frequently normal daylight is not adequate for high-quality action photography. Therefore, flash photography is an important method of producing good exposures.

Super High-Speed Flash

A popping balloon or an ice cube falling into a cocktail glass can produce highly unusual pictures. An egg breaking, or your children's water balloons exploding, are events that take place at such a high speed that the human eye is not capable of seeing the individual phases.

However, each individual phase of a process in motion can be captured by flash photography and made visible. Super high-speed flash shots, which until recently could only be made by specialists, can now be taken easily with any SLR camera and a computerized flash unit. This is possible because a computerized flash unit, which measures its own light reflected by the subject and cuts off the flash when necessary, has a flash duration between 1/500 and 1/2000 second at normal shooting distances and as short as 1/10,000 or even 1/40,000 second in the close-up range.

This is fast enough to capture almost any movement. Because the camera is too slow for such high speeds, it is easiest to take exposures in a dark environment with the shutter open, and to trigger the flash with a trigger device actuated by sound or light. A clever photographer can build or purchase an acoustic flash release device quite inexpensively. It ensures that the flash is fired when the balloon bursts or when the ice cube splashes into the water.

Such exposures require mounting the camera on a tripod and locking the shutter open with the bulb setting and a cable release. After each shot, close the shutter and advance the film, then prepare for the next picture and open the camera shutter again in the dark *(See also Light and Sound Triggers, page 146).*

Using Flash in Low Ambient Light

With TTL control: The camera is set to the desired aperture and the shutter speed set to "B" or "bulb" in the camera's manual camera exposure mode. (Use manual focus with AF cameras.) When a flash exposure is taken in very low ambient light or even in complete darkness in TTL mode, the moving object is recorded only during the relatively short duration of the flash.

Fully manual control: This requires total darkness. The camera shutter is opened for a given period of time using the bulb setting and a locking cable release. The Metz flash is set on "M" and triggered via the test flash button. Then the shutter is closed. The distance from the (preferably off-camera) flash unit to the subject was adjusted to match the selected aperture. If possible, a series of bracketed exposures should be made by increasing and decreasing the aperture setting or decreasing the manual power output ratios.

Creating Motion Blurs

When using flash, motion blurs may be created intentionally. The flash image which is sharp due to the brief duration of the flash exposure is superimposed over a second, blurred available light image taken at a slow shutter speed. This can produce very interesting results.

Motion blurs: Wherever motion is a component, fill flash may be used to create streaks. What makes this effect fascinating is the combination of sharpness and blur. For example, dancing people at a disco are a blend of sharp and unsharp, creating a strong impression of motion. At a track meet, the runner at the start creates motion streaks, as do many other subjects such as moving cars, playing children, rotating carousels, rushing pedestrians, etc. The time when the flash is fired during the long exposure determines whether the motion streaks appear in front of the subject or behind it. Normally the flash is fired at the beginning of an exposure, but this means the motion streaks lead forward from the sharp image and tend to make it appear as though it were moving backwards. A preferable effect is possible with certain models of Nikon, Canon EOS, Contax, and Pentax SLRs, which allow firing the flash just before the end of the exposure instead of at the beginning. This is flash synchronization with the second shutter curtain, commonly called "second curtain sync" Using this technique, the slow ambient light exposure creates motion streaks due to subject movement; then, at the end, the sharp flash exposure is added. This means the motion streaks are placed behind

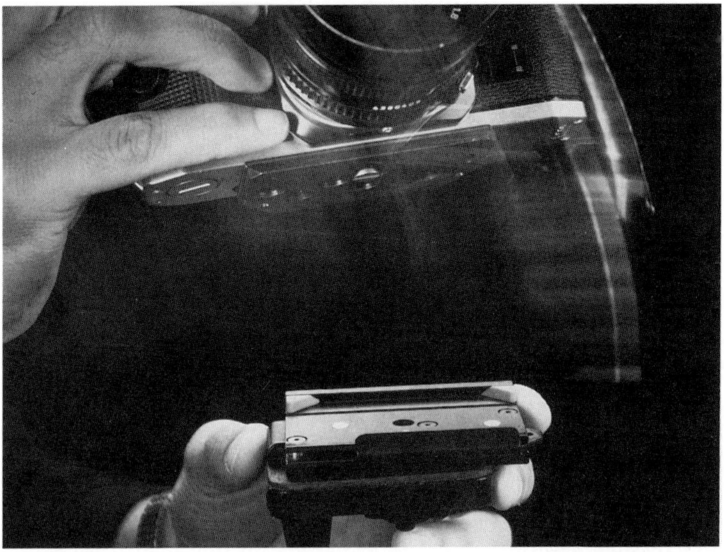

This product shot for the Stroboframe Camera Auto Quick Release is an example of effective use of motion blur. Photo: Mike McWilliams

the sharp image of the subject, a much more natural effect that can be "read" more easily by the viewer.

How to create motion blurs: For example, with a shutter speed setting of 1/8 second. During the flash exposure (approximately 1/1000 second or greater) the subject is "frozen" by the intense, short light of the flash. However, the subject is also illuminated additionally by normal ambient light during the entire 1/8 second exposure. With a moving subject, its sharp flash image will be superimposed with a second out-of-focus ambient light image. Also, if the shutter speed is slow, you can intentionally cause the blur by moving the camera with the action. Depending on the camera model, similar effects can be attained with weak ambient light when programmed autoflash or aperture priority and slow synchronization are used.

Using second curtain sync: When using slow shutter speeds, cameras that offer second shutter curtain sync should be switched to this setting. (Check with your camera's instruction manual or the appropriate *Magic Lantern Guide.*) In practice this means that the ambient light exposure occurs before the release of the flash. This effect is obvious only with slow shutter speeds, noticeable ambient light, and moving objects.

Certainly the most suitable mode for slow shutter speeds is shutter priority, or manual exposure adjustment. This situation often requires testing and practice before the best results are obtained.

Using second curtain sync to soften the flash: In addition to its use for blurred-motion pictures, second curtain sync can soften the effect of lighting that would otherwise be harsh. When a low-level ambient light exposure is made first, it can reduce contrast, while the flash adds a subtle punch.

Motion Sequences with Stroboscopic Flash

With the "strobe flash" mode offered by the Metz Mecablitz 40 MZ 2, several images of a moving object can appear in the same picture by making several flashes in rapid succession. In sports and science, stroboscopic exposures permit the analysis of rapid motion. Because strobe mode fires many flashes in rapid succession, only a partial light output is available, from a maximum of 1/4 power down to a minimum of 1/256 power.

Shooting distance, exposure and flash power: The flash unit displays the shooting distance for correct exposure at the set aperture, as well as the selected power reduction. The shooting distance can be increased either by using a larger f/stop or by using faster film. The aperture value indicated on the flash unit must be set on the camera's lens.

Flash frequency and exposure time: A flash frequency from 1 to 40 hertz (flashes per second) can be selected, which determines the interval between flashes. You must also decide how many flashes you wish to use in each exposure - a number between 1 and 20. However, a computation table may be required here. If the flash rate is 1 Hz and the number of flashes selected is 20, the exposure time must be greater than 20 seconds to include all 20 flashes in a single exposure. If you set a flash rate of 40 Hz and want to use 20 flashes, the exposure time would have to be 1/2 second.

Mecablitz 40 MZ 2 programs: Preset programs 7 and 8 of the Mecablitz 40 MZ 2 are very practical for your first tries at strobe techniques. Program 7 provides a partial light output of 1/8, a flash number of 5, a frequency of 1 Hz, a shutter speed of 8 seconds, and an aperture of f/5.6. Program 8 sets an output of 1/32 for 10 flashes, a frequency of 5 Hz, a shutter speed of 2 seconds, and an aperture of f/5.6. In both cases, the zoom reflector should be set to 50mm and film speed is 100 ISO. (These programs can be deleted or customized at the user's discretion.)

These settings apply to a dark background or a background sufficiently far behind the subject to appear dark. If a flash sequence results in more than three overlapping images of the main subject, you must make an exposure correction - as with any multiple-exposure technique - by setting a minus correction.

For each stroboscopic sequence, all of the following adjustments are required:

1. Adjust the camera to "M" and set the shutter speed. Slow shutter speeds or the bulb setting may be selected in total darkness. In this case, an out-of-focus "ghost image" caused by ambient light will not occur.
2. Switch on the flash unit.
3. Check the ISO film speed setting.
4. Press the N-button on the flash unit (alternate function of the ISO-button).
5. Set the number of flashes using the plus or minus buttons.
6. Press the f-button for Hz (alternate function of the buzzer button).
7. Select the desired frequency number with the plus or minus buttons.
8. Check and, if necessary, adjust the partial light output.
9. Press the aperture button. Check whether the adjusted aperture and the indicated maximum distance correspond to the actual distance of the subject; otherwise change this with the plus or minus button.
10. Set the required f/stop on the lens.

A:

Picture a: By using a different approach, an otherwise boring subject becomes more interesting. Different color filters were attached to three flash units to photograph this screw.

Picture b: The camera was mounted on a tripod in a dark room, the shutter locked opened on the "bulb" setting. The flash unit attached to a sound trigger was tripped by the shot from the air gun. The only problem was to determine the time delay between the shot and the bursting of the balloon.

B:

This is a very successful example of a stroboscopic exposure made with a Mecablitz 40 MZ 2 unit. The challenge here was to correctly expose the overlapping images.

C:

Another example of a stroboscopic exposure. The time between flashes was increased and the number of flashes per exposure was decreased compared to Plate B.

D:

High-speed shots such as these are obtained by connecting the flash unit to a sound trigger. The camera shutter is locked open using the "bulb" setting in a darkened room. The flash is triggered by the sound of the shattering light bulb. Several flash units, fitted with different color filters, were used for illumination.

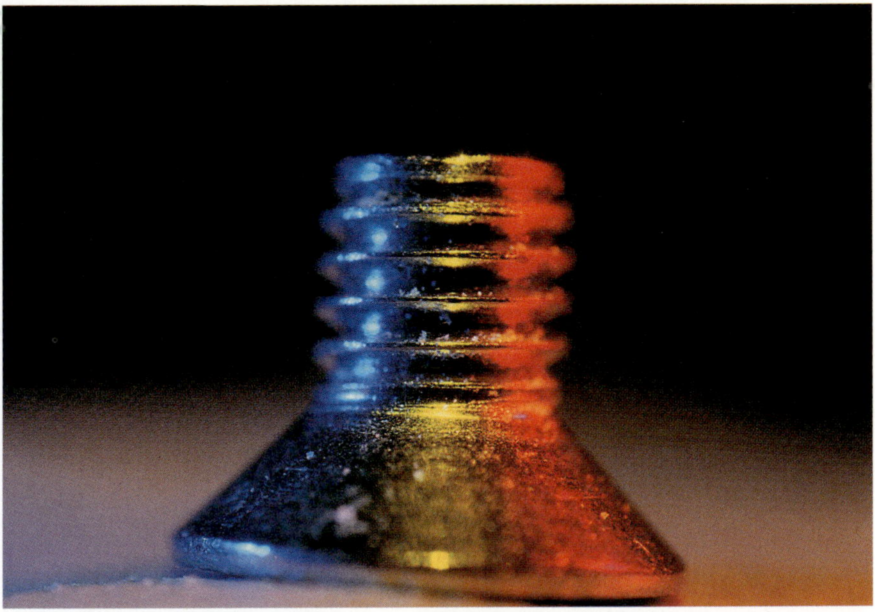

a

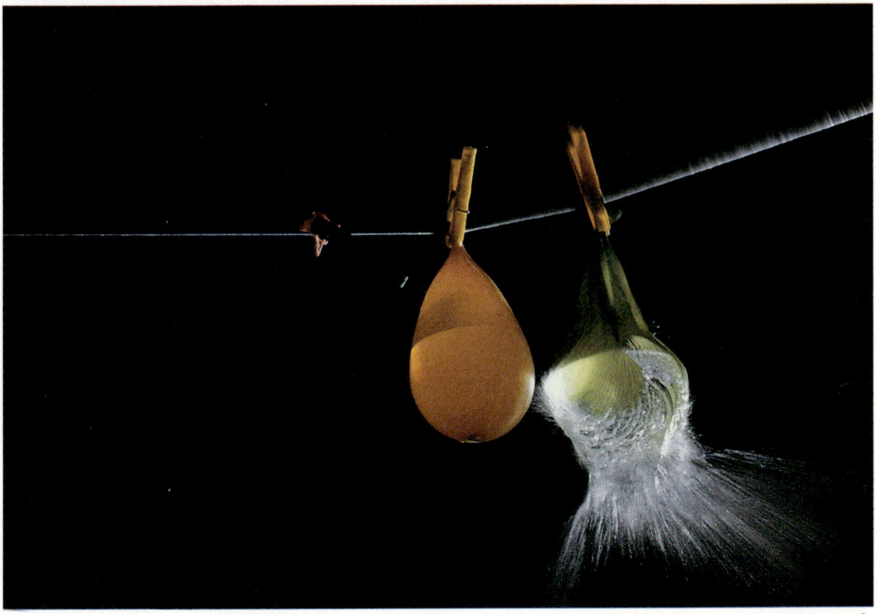

b

– Tafel A –

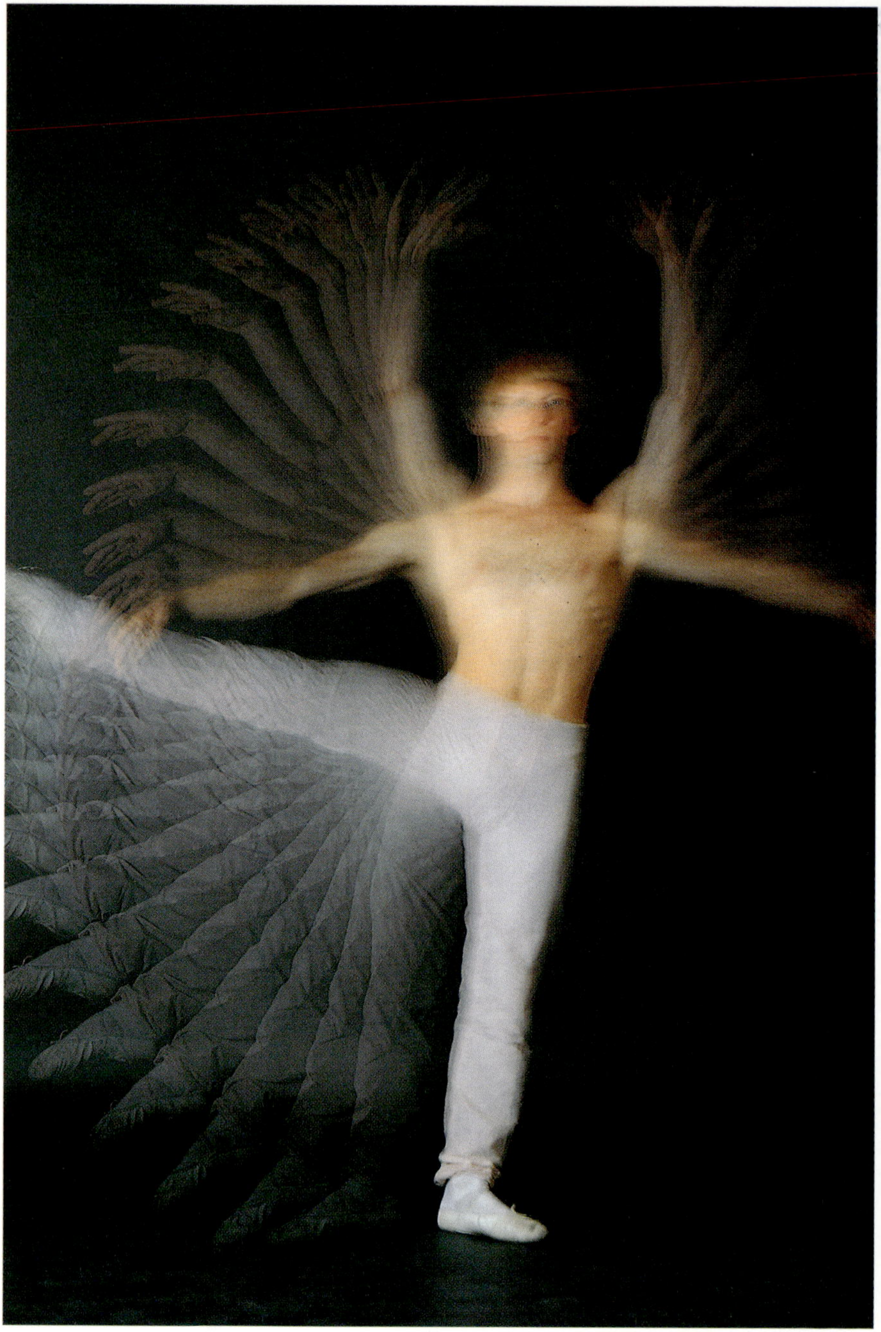

– Tafel B –

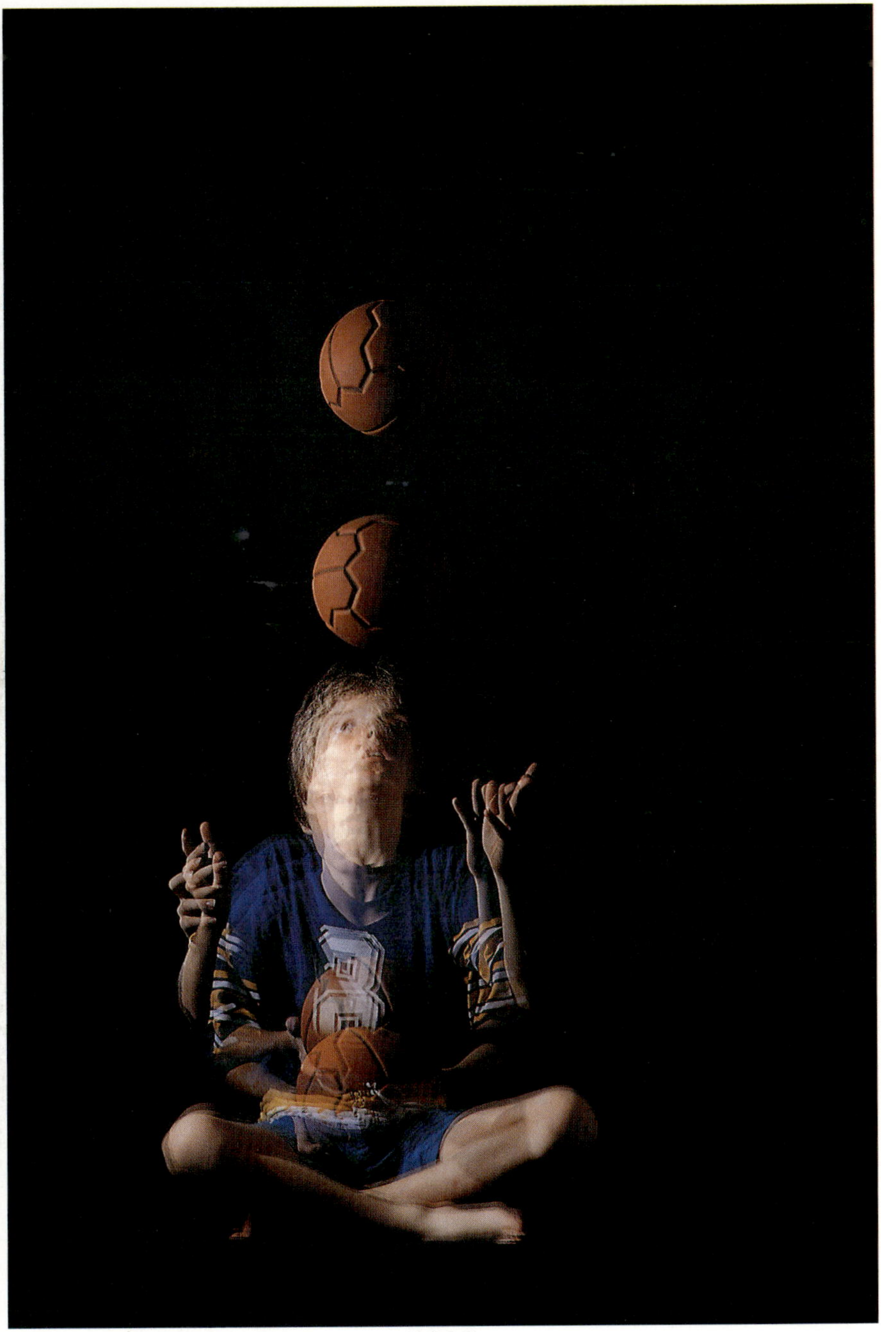

– Tafel C –

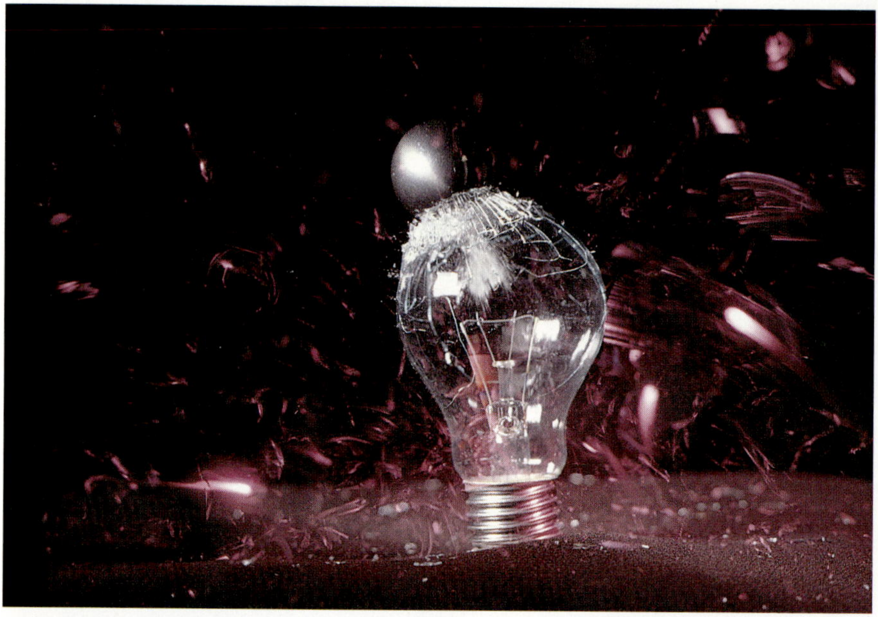

a

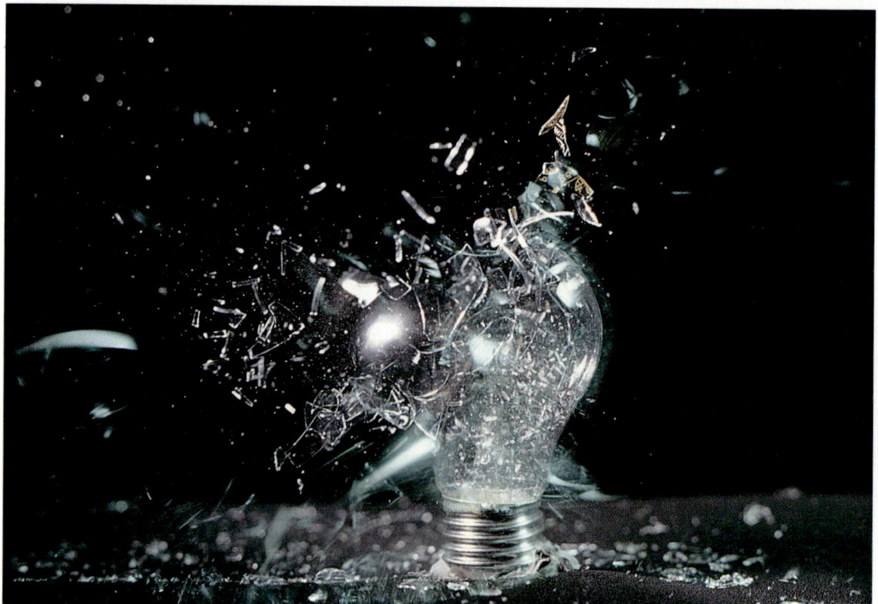

b

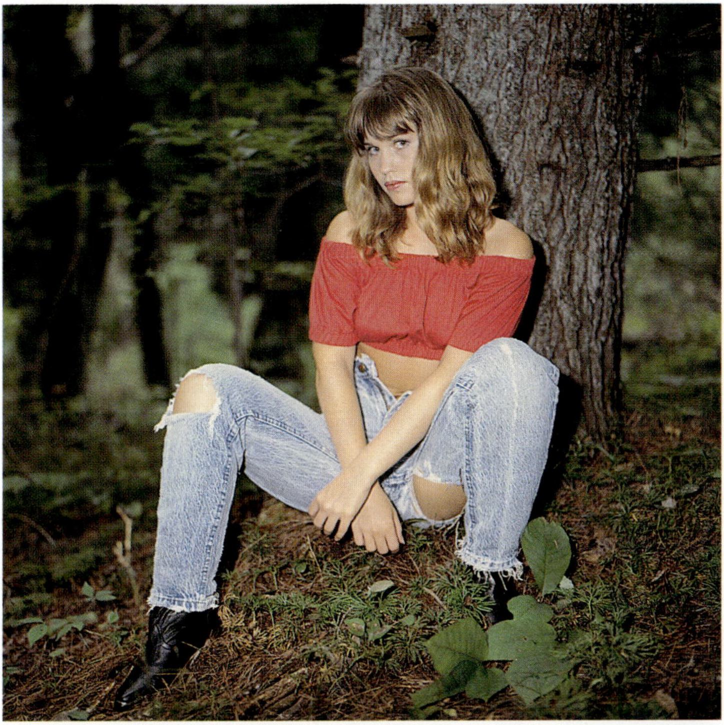

a

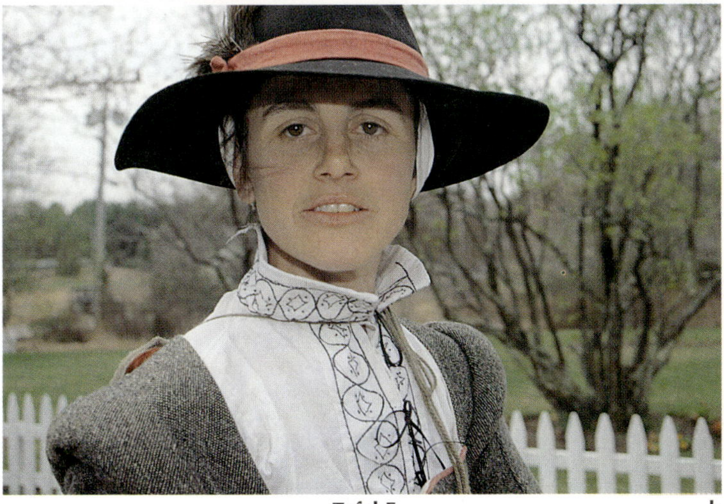

– Tafel E –

b

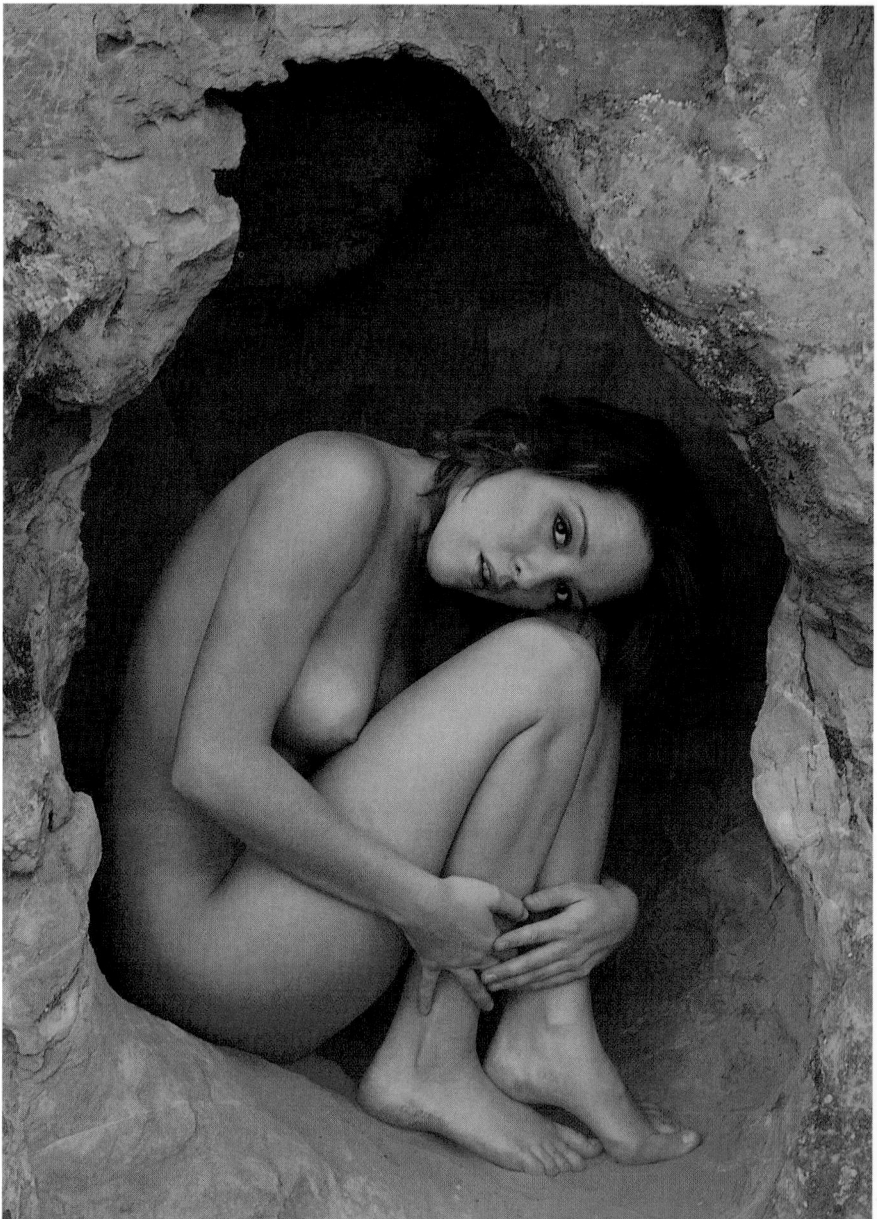

– Tafel F –

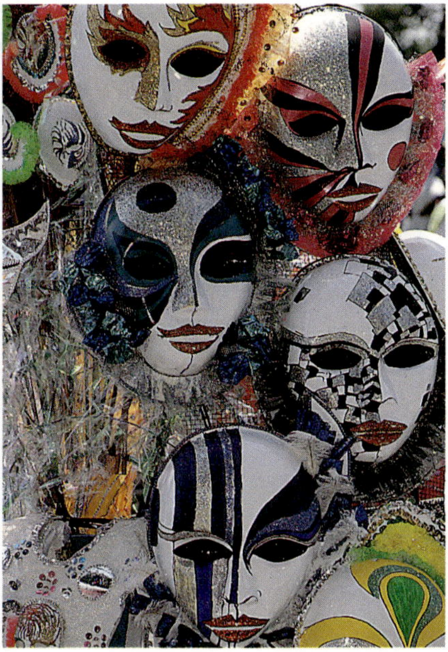
a

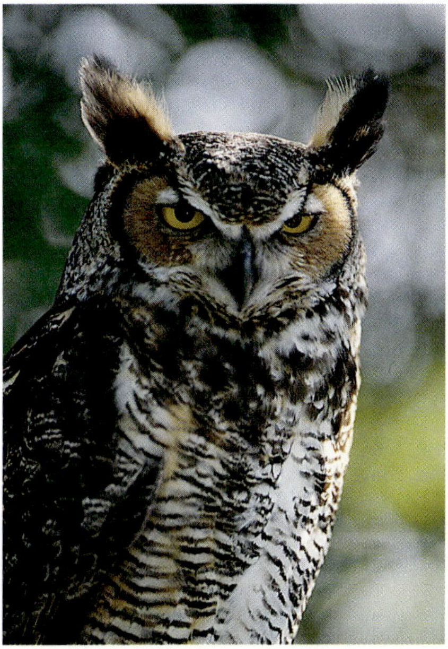
b

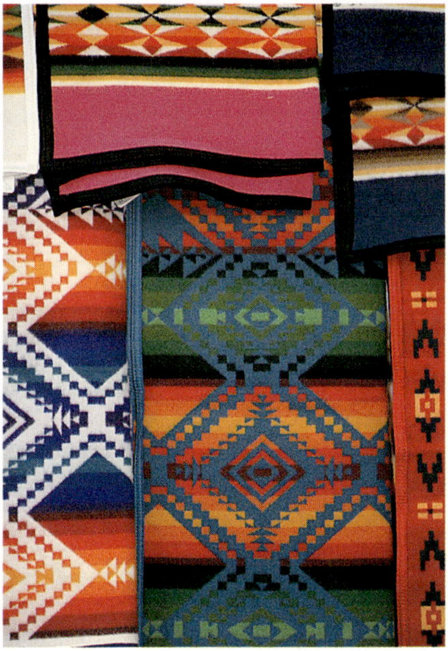
c

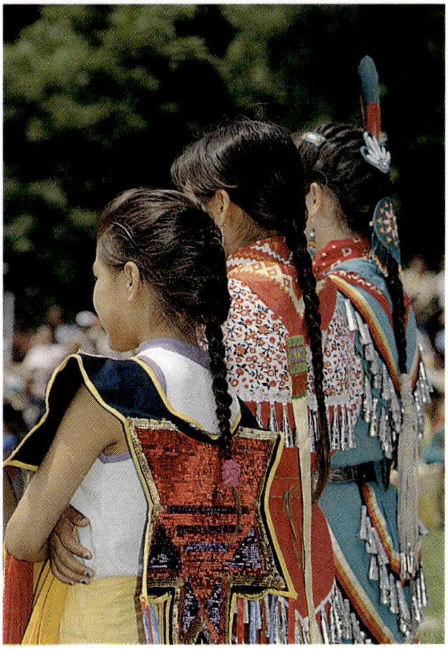
d

– Tafel G –

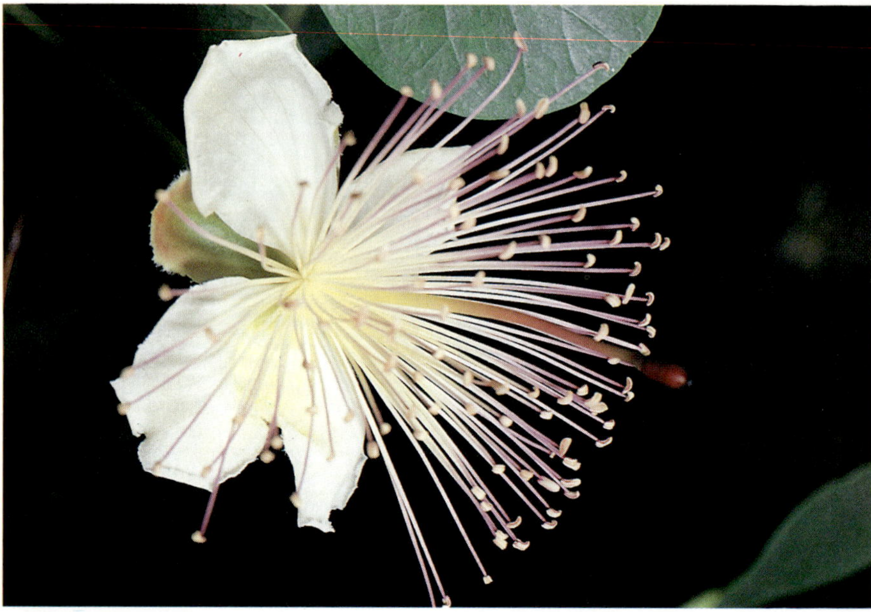

a

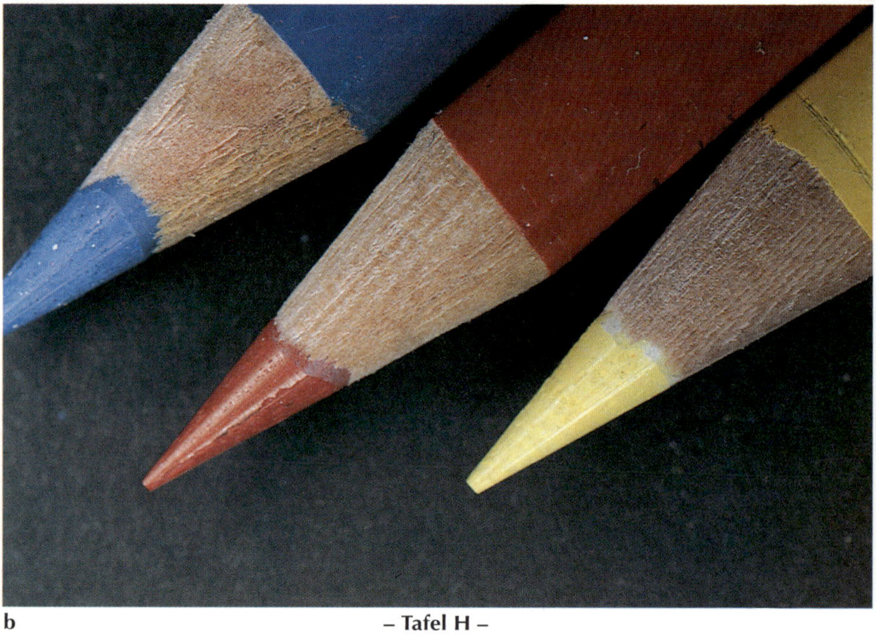

b

– Tafel H –

E:
Both pictures were taken under an overcast sky. The flash provided intense colors and the impression of sunshine. If the camera does not have automatic fill flash control, the aperture set on the flash unit should be one f/stop greater than that set on the lens in order to obtain a bright, natural lighting effect. Photo a: Bob Shell.

F:
This picture was shot with off-camera flash and a reflector screen to provide the appropriate amount of fill. The flash effect is hardly noticeable and a pleasingly warm, natural mood was created. Photo: Bob Shell.

G:
Every exposure in this series received its brilliant colors from supplementary fill-flash. The setting for the flash unit was one f/stop less than the lens aperture to maintain the mood created by natural light. Photos: Peter K. Burian

H:
The use of flash is indispensable in the close-up range in order to achieve apertures which are sufficiently small for the required depth of field. For subjects such as these, an external sensor positioned close to the subject is recommended.

Improving Results with Bounce Flash

Typical flash pictures with harsh lighting and unpleasant shadows are the result of a combination of two factors, a point-light source and direct frontal illumination.

The simplest way out of this photographic dilemma is to use bounce flash, possibly even with the use of an additional reflector card for filling in deep shadows. But what should be done to improve results if the photographer must use frontal light because the surroundings are much too dark or there is not a suitable surface to bounce the flash light off?

Better Bounce Flash with Metz Twin-head Flash

Manufacturers of flash equipment are more than familiar with the problems of direct flash illumination. For example, a shoe-mounted flash is the easiest way to provide enough light for mak-

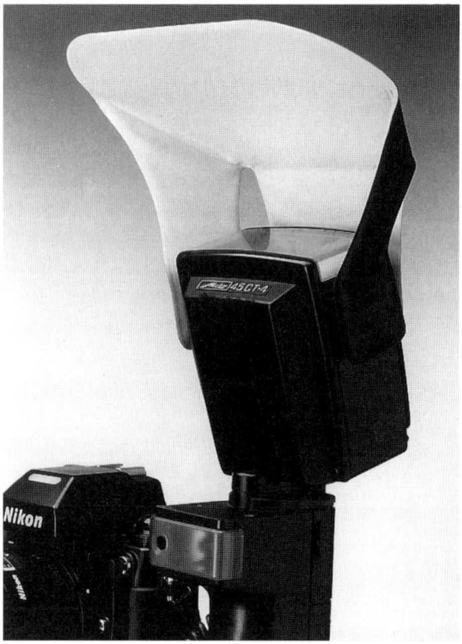

This reflector by Lumiquest®, fastened to the swivel/tilt flash head of a 45 CT 4, softens the light considerably. The smaller flash located on the handle may be activated to provide fill-flash.

ing snapshots, action shots, or whenever quick reaction time is imperative. But the same convenience can often be achieved with much better lighting quality by using a "twin-head" flash with a bounce card or reflector. The Metz Mecablitz 45 CL 4 flash unit, the compact 40 MZ 2 flash, and several other Metz flash units have a second flash head below the main flash head. This may be switched on or off separately providing direct fill light when the main head is tilted up for bounce.

Secondary fill with bounce flash: The secondary flash should be used whenever the main flash is used for bounce lighting, especially when using a ceiling or wall as the bounce surface. The small secondary flash head provides 10 to 15% of the total light output, aimed directly at the subject. The remaining 85 to 90% of the light comes from the main flash. Together, the twin heads provide soft overall lighting. The main light is bounced off the ceiling and the direct fill-lighting reduces the shadows under the chin and in the eye sockets, and creates the important catchlights in the subject's eyes.

Lighting balance: The lighting balance between the two flash heads varies, due to variations in bouncing the light from the main reflector. Depending on the distance from the flash unit to the "bounce" surface and the amount of diffusion of the light caused by the surface, there will be an illumination loss of 1 to 3 f/stops. The greater the diffusion of the main light, the stronger the relative effect of the light from the secondary flash head. For example, if there is a relative brightness difference between the two flash heads of three stops; i.e. the main head puts out sufficient light for f/8, the secondary flash head emits light for f/2.8.

Automatic TTL adjustment of output: If the light loss due to bouncing the light from the ceiling is 50% (one f/stop), the main head's output increases until the flash unit's sensor or TTL meter has detected sufficient light for the selected aperture. The main head's output increases by one f/stop to compensate for the light lost from bouncing. In this case the output of the secondary flash head also increases proportionately, so its light also becomes twice as strong. The brightness difference between the main head and secondary head is now only two f/stops instead of three. If the reflecting surface were to cause a light loss of two f/stops, which is not unusual, the difference in output between the two heads would be reduced to just one f/stop.

Adjusting the fill light: When the loss of light due to bouncing the flash reaches three f/stops — for instance, from a high ceiling — the secondary flash head becomes as bright as the bounced main light. However, you may not want this much fill-in light, so Metz supplies two light-reducing filters for use on the secondary flash head. The filters reduce the flash output by 25 or 50%, thus reducing the fill light by one to two f/stops.

Twin-head technique: It's important to aim the main head correctly when bouncing the flash off walls or the ceiling. When photographing a subject at a distance of approximately 3 to 6 feet, you should aim the main head straight up (90 degrees). However, at greater distances, up to about 12 feet, you should tilt the head upward by only 60 degrees — that is, aimed up and somewhat ahead of you. When photographing subjects that are even farther away, aim the main head at a point on the ceiling or wall about one-third of the distance from the flash to the subject. In all cases, remember that light is reflected from the bounce surface at an angle equal to the angle at which it strikes the surface. In technical terms: the angle of incidence is equal to the angle of reflection.

Bounce considerations: Not all ceilings and walls can be used as bounce surfaces. Colored surfaces, dark ceilings, and wooden ceilings or walls are not suitable. Neither are very high ceilings or distant walls. When you use bounce flash, be careful that the complete distance that the light travels is within the maximum range of your flash unit. The direct distance from the flash unit to the subject is not important. Maximum range must cover the total distance from the flash unit to the reflecting surface and from there to the subject. You must also allow for the loss of light caused by diffusion and absorption by the bounce surface when you calculate the maximum range for your flash unit.

Advantages of the Metz twin-head design: The Metz twin-head design offers greater lighting control and quality. If you aim the main head upward and use the optional Metz reflector, the loss of light due to bouncing remains constant and predictable. Using this simple method means the main head provides soft, indirect lighting and a more gradual fall-off of brightness in the farther areas of the room; always a more appealing lighting effect. The secondary head creates catchlights in the subject's eyes and enhances the brightness of colors.

Reflectors with twin-head bounce: Even though the soft, indirect lighting created by bouncing the light from a ceiling or wall offers obvious advantages, a reflector mounted on the flash unit is definitely easier to control. The light is not diffused as softly, but you can be sure the reflected light will really reach the subject. That is important in a fast-moving shooting situation such as a wedding. When you're concentrating on your subject, it's all too easy to accidentally aim the flash at a doorway or a window where all the light disappears, never to be seen again. Also, using a reflector mounted on the flash unit provides the soft lighting effect of bounce flash outdoors or in large halls, where the ceiling and walls cannot be used.

No matter what technique you use for bounce flash, be sure the angle covered by the flash is sufficient. To be sure of this, set the flash reflector for a focal length shorter than the focal length of the camera lens, or use the optional wide-angle diffuser on the flash.

Off-Camera Flash with Metz SCA System Flash Units

Stroboframe® Flash Brackets

Most professional photographers prefer the results of off-camera flash with a professional flash bracket such as those manufactured by Stroboframe®

Advantages of using a flash bracket: Professional, natural-appearing illumination can be achieved with Metz Mecablitz flash units by positioning the flash high above the lens. Light has a more natural effect (like sunlight) when it comes from above. Flash units mounted directly on or next to the camera produce unflattering light with harsh shadows. With a bracket centered high over the lens harsh shadows fall below and behind the subject. The prob-

The Stroboframe SQ2000 bracket holds the flash high and centered above the lens.

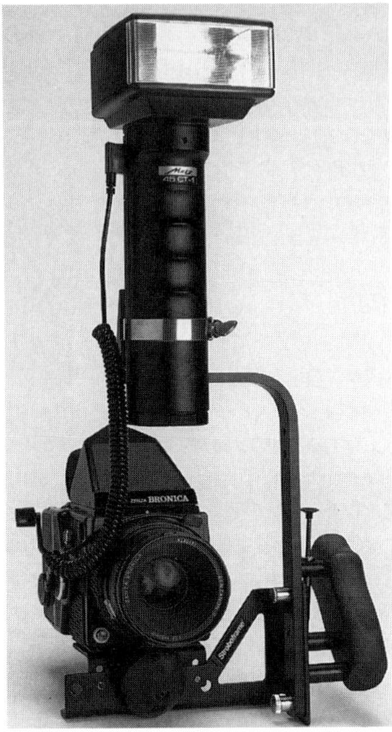

lem of red-eye becomes more pronounced the closer the flash head is to the optical axis. This problem is also solved by using a bracket which positions the Metz flash unit high above the camera.

Stroboframe and Metz system flashes: Stroboframe offers a large number of flash brackets and adapter plates for 35mm and medium format cameras. These may be used to position the flash unit as desired while the camera position may be changed between vertical and horizontal formats. All Stroboframe flash brackets accept a shoe-style flash mount to accommodate compact Metz Mecablitz units. Stroboframe offers a Metz Quick Release Flash Mount which is compatible with the "handle-mount" receptacle found on the collar of Mecablitz 45 CT 4 and 60 CL 4. The professional Stroboframe flash brackets included in this chapter are modularly designed. All can be fitted with these interchangeable flash mounts and other Stroboframe accessories. Stroboframe flash brackets are designed to provide a well-balanced union of flash and camera, even with larger flash units such as the Mecablitz 60 CL 4.

System 2000 flash brackets: These are particularly compact in design and intended for diverse applications. The *RL2000 Rotary Link Flash Bracket* consists of a patented movable camera platform which allows an instant adjustment of the camera to horizontal or vertical format, while the flash unit's position remains unchanged. The *SQ2000 Square Format Bracket* for cameras with square image format or cameras with rotating film magazines is fitted with a fixed camera plate.

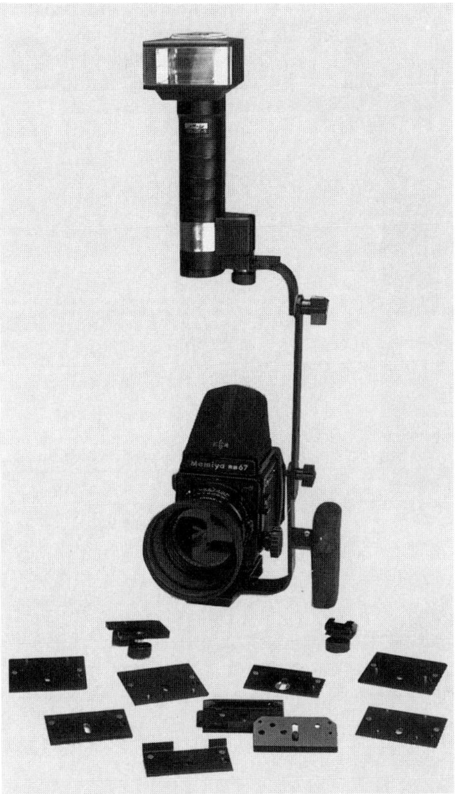

All Stroboframe brackets mentioned, including the R66b bracket shown, are compatible with the full line of Stroboframe accessories.

R-series brackets: The R-series flash brackets are large and sturdy. They are designed for larger cameras or photographers who prefer a larger bracket and they permit even greater distances between camera and flash. The R4b has the same rotary-link camera platform as the RL2000 model while the R66b bracket is intended for cameras with square image format or rotating film magazines.

Pro-T bracket: The Pro-T bracket is simpler and more compact than either the 2000 series or R-series brackets. It allows the photographer to hold the camera as though no bracket were attached while still offering optimum flash positioning. Rather than use a camera rotating mechanism, the Pro-T has a pivoting

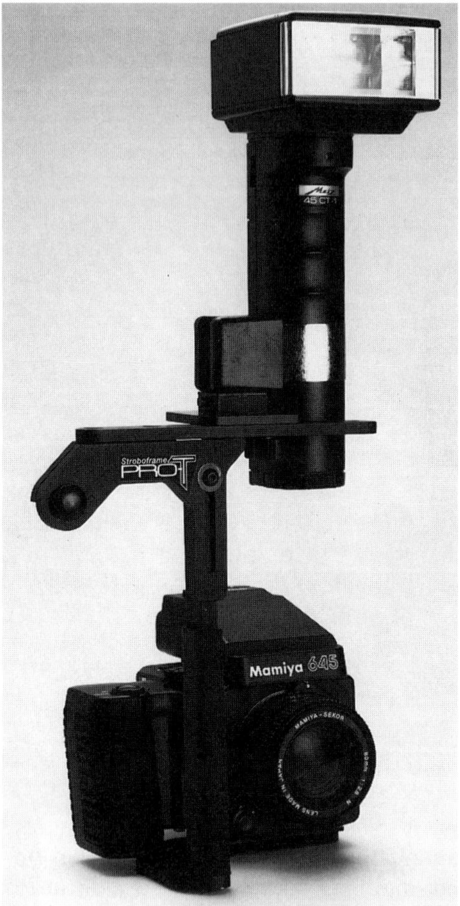

The Stroboframe Pro-T is a versatile flash bracket designed for comfort, fast handling, and optimum flash placement.

flash arm to center the flash over the lens while the camera is turned vertically.

Using a Metz SCA System Flash on a Bracket

In order to mount any Metz flash on a bracket, the proper SCA system connecting cord must be used to maintain the camera/flash dedicated features. The following is an overview of what is required. (Also see Chapter 2, SCA Accessories)

SCA Cords and connectors: The simplest method is to connect the camera and the flash unit by using a cord which mounts on the hot shoe of the camera. The SCA 300 and 3000 Systems provide coiled cords which connect the hot-shoe adapter and the flash unit The new generation of Minolta Maxxum/Dynax xi, Canon EOS and Nikon AF cameras use the SCA 3007 A cord with the SCA 3000 System. This is connected to the hot-shoe contacts of the camera where the SCA Adapter is mounted, thereby maintaining full control. As a result, all flash modes and automatic functions are available.

Standard PC connection with the SCA system: Should the camera used for flash exposures have a non-dedicated hot shoe with only a single contact, the SCA dedicated connectors are of no use since the features offered cannot be utilized. The photographer should use a normal PC sync cord. To allow this, the special shoe on the SCA flash unit must be exchanged for a standard SCA 301 which has only one contact. A sync cord which has a jack connector on one end and a PC connector on the other is plugged in to the outlet on the side of the SCA 301 foot and the PC plug on the cord is plugged in to the standard sync terminal on the camera.

Sync cords for handle-mount Metz flashes: Comparable sync cords are available for handle-mount flash units. Instead of a jack connector, these cords have a special handle connector fitting all SCA 300 handle-mount flash units with the exception of the 60 CT 1.

Final comments: In most situations, the combination of an off-camera flash with a second flash, or even an indirect off-camera flash will provide a technically balanced result. In so doing, shadows are largely eliminated and an impression of directed light remains. The off-camera flash may be used easily as auxiliary flash to augment normal exposure. New flash techniques such as fill flash have certainly made the off-camera flash in its original form less important. In many instances it is no longer necessary to provide the picture with a desired mood by using flash units in an unconventional way. Standard metering technology with a touch of flash, enhances pictures technically without any changes to the effect created by the ambient light.

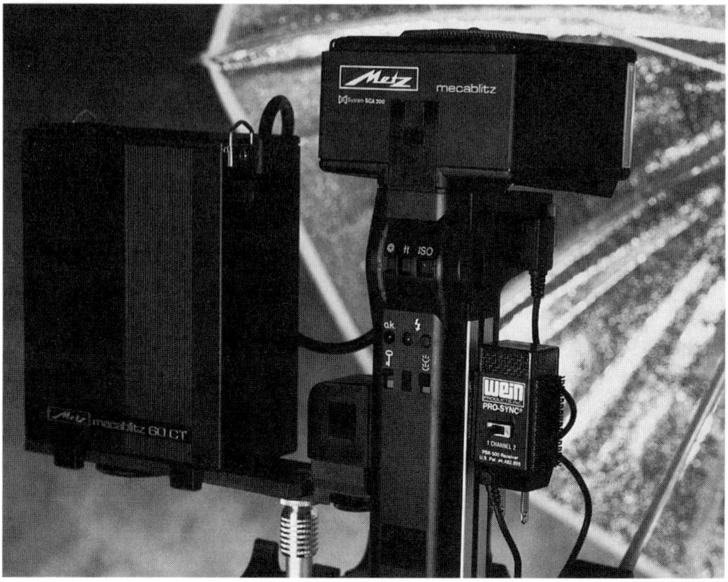

Remote control systems like the Wein Pro-Sync Infrared Pro-Sync, make it possible to fire the flash unit without cords or interference from other photographer's flash. (Shown: 2-channel Pro-Sync receiver on a Metz 60 CT 4)

Remote Triggering of Flash

The Saunders Group distributes the remote flash triggers (often called slave units) made by Wein Products. There are many models, giving photographers their choice of a variety of configurations and sensitivity levels, depending on the need. Wein also makes high-quality infrared remote flash triggering systems, useful for a wide variety of applications.

Light and Sound Flash Triggers

A light barrier consists of a light-emitting source and a receiver. When the beam of light shining on the receiver is interrupted, an electronic switch triggers the camera or the flash.

Many kinds of photocells can be used to make a light barrier. The external Metz Mecalux 11 sensor is excellent for initial experiments. Entire kits and complete light barriers are offered by a number of electronics firms. Author, Bob Shell, has had considerable experience and exceptional results from the English-made Mazof equipment, which allows very fine tuning of the sensitivity and has a built-in adjustable delay for precise flash timing. It can be also used as a sound trigger and a vibration sensor so sensitive it can be triggered by a butterfly landing on a twig.

Working with Multiple Flash Units

Image quality can be significantly improved just by using two flash units, one as the main light source and the second for fill light. There is a simple reason for this. Unlike the human eye, film cannot handle extreme brightness differences correctly. Once a certain level of contrast has been exceeded, the light areas will appear too light and dark areas will appear black. Therefore, additional light sources are used to compensate for the limitations of photographic materials. A second flash also adds a modeling effect, giving the subject more definition and a more natural appearance.

Professional photographers are well aware of this, and quality-conscious amateur photographers should also try this technique. Today's photographic technology makes using multiple flash units as easy as child's play. The following discussion covers techniques applicable to all cameras, with or without TTL metering. Wireless TTL mode will be discussed later.

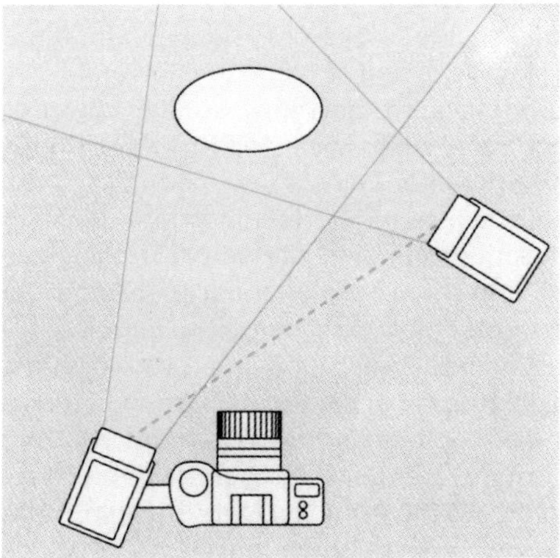

An effective lighting setup is created when the main flash is on-camera and when the secondary unit is directed at the subject from slightly above at an angle of approximately 45°. The secondary light should be set to output 1 to 3 stops less light.

Using Wireless Systems

The inconvenient connecting wires that were formerly needed when using multiple flash units are no longer required with today's wireless multiple flash systems. Metz offers the Mecalux slave flash and the Mecamat, which allow the main flash to trigger several additional flash units without any wire connections. As illustrated, this makes it easy to obtain professional results.

With TTL: Owners of cameras with TTL metering should be aware that these systems take the light from all flash units into account, provided they are fired simultaneously.

With automatic mode: Even those who take pictures only with the flash unit in automatic mode, or who utilize existing light in automatic mode, can easily determine the ratio of the main flash to slave flash. The slave flash is used in telecomputer mode and the lens aperture is closed down by 1/2 to 1 f/stop smaller than the slave flash unit indicates. This prevents the fill light from becoming dominant; it will only have a brightening effect.

As an example: The camera lens is adjusted to the automatic aperture required by the main light, for example f/8, while the slave unit is set to a wider aperture such as f/5.6, meaning the slave will provide one stop less light than the main light. If the slave unit does not offer the desired aperture, you will need to set the main flash and the lens aperture based on the output of the slave flash; if the slave requires f/4, set the main flash and lens aperture to f/5.6.

A two-flash setup can provide direct lighting on the subject or can create a special mood, and what works with two flash units also works with three or more units.

One problem can arise when using multiple flash units in automatic mode. Small flash units (nearly all compact units) have a much shorter flash duration than handle-mount units, and the very short duration may cause color shifts due to reciprocity failure. If compact units and handle-mount units are used together, the areas illuminated by the compact units may show a color shift, while areas illuminated by the handle-mount units will not, resulting in fluctuations of tone and color throughout the picture. One way to avoid this is to set the compact units for maximum light output which makes their flash duration longer.

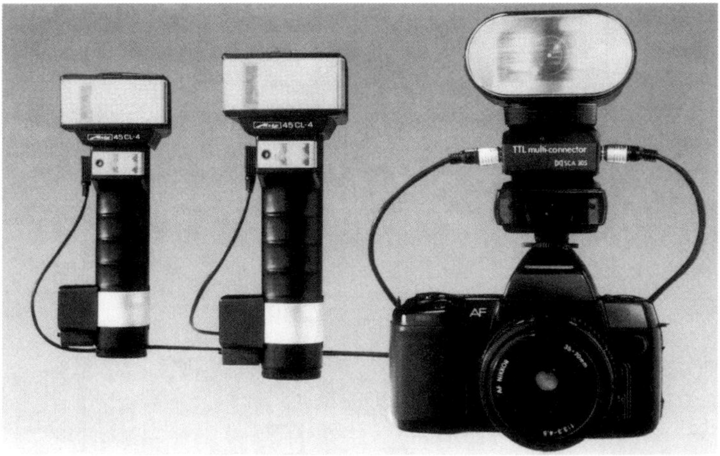

The TTL Multiconnector System SCA 305 A directly controls several SCA 300 System flash units. By combining several Multiconnectors, up to seven flash units may be controlled by the camera's TTL flash meter.

Using the TTL Multiconnector SCA 305

An easy-to-use, professional lighting setup can be created using several SCA flash units and an SLR camera with TTL flash metering. With this system, the camera's TTL metering can control all the flash units by means of the Metz TTL Multiconnector SCA 305. With this, the exposure-control signals from the camera are transferred through the SCA Adapter to the flash units, and the signals sent back to the camera by the flash units. For example, the signals indicating flash readiness, are sent to the adapter interface. A Multiconnector is capable of coordinating the work of three SCA flash units. If required, additional multiconnectors can be attached in "cascade" fashion.

For even further distances: The Multiconnector can be a considerable distance away from the flash unit. The 15 foot (5 m) extension cable SCA 306 VA can be used between the Multiconnector and the flash unit, and as many as three cables can be connected to each other, which should be adequate for nearly any lighting situation.

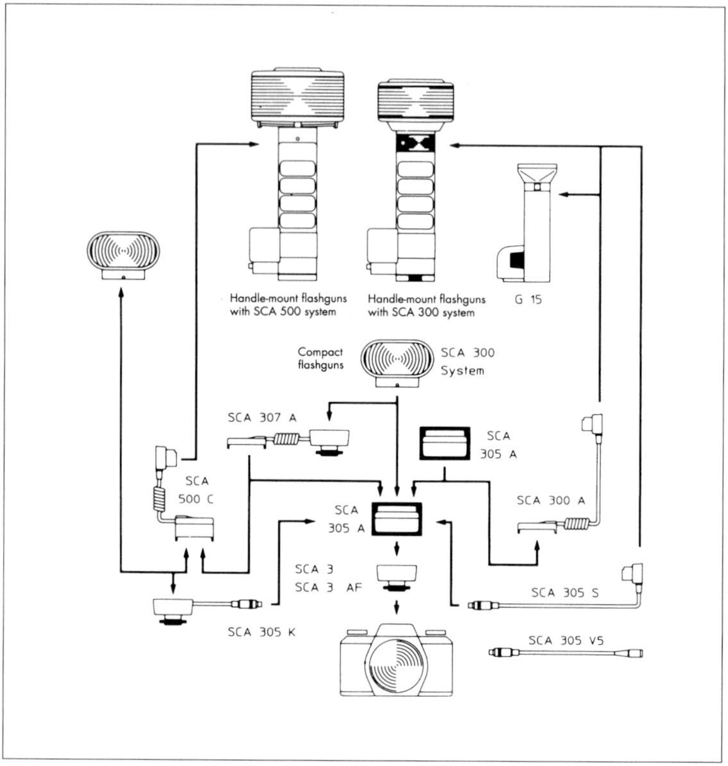

This overview shows all of the options for combining SCA units using the various adapters and connectors of the TTL Multiconnector SCA 305 System.

Using TTL Multiconnectors: The TTL Multiconnector is about the same size as most SCA Adapters. First the SCA Adapter is attached to the camera; then the Multiconnector is used to connect the individual flash units with each other. There are several adapter cables for connecting the Multiconnector and the flash units. The SCA 305 K is for compact flash units, while the SCA 305 S is for handle-mount units.

Setting up the system: When setting up the system it is important to connect all the flash units together first. Next, connect them to the camera, and last, switch them on. Once all the connections have been established, the flash readiness of all flash units may be tested on the Multiconnector itself and in the camera's viewfinder display. Successful firing of flashes may also be verified on the Multiconnector and on the camera, if it offers that feature.

Allow time for full recharging: It is a good idea to give the flash units a few extra seconds to recycle after the flash readiness indicator begins to blink, because this indicates only 70% of full charge. Otherwise, problems with faulty exposures could result if full flash power is required.

TTL metering is particularly convenient for special situations such as studio illumination, because no computation is necessary. However, as with all flash modes, you still have to correct the aperture when the subject's reflectance is unusually high or low. As already mentioned, the most frequent errors are caused by light surfaces or strongly reflecting objects, which cause the flash unit to reduce the light output excessively, producing underexposed photographs. Unusually dark subjects can create the opposite problem – overexposure.

TTL OTF flash should never be tested without film in the camera because the camera's metering cell reads the light reflected from the film, and reading the light from the camera's pressure plate, when there is no film in the camera, will cause exposure errors because film has a lower reflectance than the pressure plate.

Causes of uneven exposures: If your pictures show uneven flash output from frame to frame, this may be due to not waiting long enough for all flash units to recycle completely. (As mentioned, the flash-ready indicator comes on at only 70% of full charge.)

When used properly, the Multiconnector is very helpful. It permits excellent, studio-like illumination. For example, the light used for fill can be soft bounce lighting and will still be controlled correctly by the metering system.

Filters can be useful: At times it may be useful to reduce the amount of light emitted by the units providing fill flash. You can do this using special light-reducing filter sets, or if you already have a filter holder, you can use a Kodak Wratten neutral density filter. It is also possible to simply use light-absorbing plastic sheet material, acetate, Letraset (black halftone) or even a piece of evenly exposed sheet film.

If your portrait photographs do not have satisfactory skin tones, try using a UV-absorbing filter, or, better yet, a skylight or warming filter to give the light a warmer color.

Other applications with the Multiconnector set-up: The Multiconnector is useful for more than portrait photography. It is equally effective for large and small still-life setups, which for the first time can look professionally lighted without the expense of a studio flash set-up.

The Multiconnector can also be used for copystand photography by attaching flash units next to the copystand's tungsten lights, which assures that the flash illumination will be as uniform as the regular copystand lighting.

Inexpensive modeling lights: Even photographers with very little experience in lighting can make effective use of flash by improvising modeling lights. These are small, inexpensive spotlights that can be clamped to the flash units and assist the photographer in previsualizing the effect of the flash.

For large rooms: To illuminate large spaces such as houses of worship, meeting halls, or even caves, several flash units can be connected together and the camera will indicate whether the exposure was adequate. Older SCA 500 System flash units can also be connected with the Multiconnector, and even a mixture of units can be used. The SCA 500 flash units require an additional system converter.

Remote-Controlled TTL Flash Operation

Metz offers this state-of-the-art control technology in the Mecablitz 40 MZ 2. The feature works with all cameras equipped with TTL flash metering and is capable of controlling two or more additional flash units via the SCA 300 or 3000 Adapter System. To do this, the camera's flash unit serves as a controller, and any number of Mecablitz 40 MZ 2 flash units can be programmed for slave operation and positioned anywhere in the room. In addition, the Mecablitz 40 MZ 2 can be fired wirelessly with the

Minolta 5200i and 5400xi flash units and with the built-in miniature units of the Minolta xi and si series. In this case, the Mecablitz 40 MZ 2 becomes the slave unit.

Using the SCA 3080 Slave Adapter: Wireless, off-camera use of the Mecablitz 40 MZ 2 flash unit first requires attaching an SCA 3080 Slave Adapter. Slave flash units can be mounted in any convenient fashion, using lightstands, tripods, flash clamps, flash holders, or monopods. Coordinating the camera and flash units to produce a carefully controlled flash is quite simple:

1. Adjust the camera to TTL flash mode and turn on the attached flash unit.
2. Set the flash unit to TTL using the mode selector switch (on the rear, bottom left side).
3. Push the Remote button on the camera flash unit.
4. By pushing the + or - button, select the data-transfer channel or controller address, Co 1 or Co 2.
5. If necessary, connect a slave adapter to the slave flash units, then follow the above steps and set up the system. Each slave unit must be switched ON individually.
6. Now press the manual release button on the flash unit; this button also activates the flash readiness display.

Slave flash units respond after a slight time delay, so you can easily verify that each unit has fired and therefore has been properly set up for wireless operation. When the remote-controlled flash unit is ready for operation, the AF flash lamp will blink and flash readiness will be indicated. The Mecablitz may additionally indicate this ready state by an optional audio alarm.

Testing the system: If you test your wireless set-up and find that a slave flash unit does not respond, this may indicate that the unit's sensor on the base plate is not accurately aligned with the camera or that it is too far away. Re-align the slave adapter and try triggering the flash again. Making a test flash is very important because it automatically sets the slave units to the correct data transfer channel (Co 1 or Co 2). In order for the slave flash to receive the control signals dependably, arrange for an unimpeded, direct line-of-sight visual connection between the camera and the slave. Be sure the subject does not block this path.

Allowing enough sync time: As soon as the camera's TTL metering system has detected a sufficient amount of light (reflected from the film surface), the on-camera flash sends a "shut-off" signal to the slave flash units. To allow sufficient time for these signals, a sync speed of 1/45 second is required, even if the camera can normally provide a faster sync speed. Wireless remote-control TTL flash metering can be used in the camera's fully automatic mode and all other modes that allow TTL flash metering and slow sync speeds.

Filters for flash control: In order to be able to take full advantage of this special flash feature you should know how much light is needed, and where and how the light will be used. As discussed in a previous section, a Metz light-reducing filter set can be used for precise control.

You can create exceptional lighting by using the rule of thumb that the fill light should be one f/stop weaker than the main light and that, to produce a bright outline, the backlight must be at the most one f/stop brighter than the main light. The exact ratio between light sources is a matter of taste and also depends on the final display; transparencies allow greater contrast differences within a picture than prints do.

An example: To create a strong side light effect, you want to attenuate the light from the camera so that it acts only as fill. By placing a light-reducing filter over the on-camera flash, you reduce its output by 50% (one f/stop) while the off-camera side light remains unaffected. These brightness differences will be discussed again later, in conjunction with close-ups and portraits.

Working distances: Practical tests have demonstrated that Metz slaves allow the flash units to be positioned without problems at distances of up to 15 feet (5 m). Indoor shots and pictures taken in soft light permit even greater working distances, so it is possible to illuminate an entire area without connecting wires.

Other advantages: But the working distance is not the main advantage, most important is being able to place your lights conveniently, without awkward wires that could trip someone. Another advantage: when taking portraits with a reduced amount of fill flash from the on-camera flash, you can change positions yet keep the same lighting, without changing the original set-up.

Special Wireless Flash Features of Minolta Cameras

Wireless remote TTL flash metering in the Metz style is also possible in combination with Minolta Maxxum/Dynax xi and si flash technology.

In this case, the Metz Mecablitz 40 MZ 2 with SCA 3301 Adapter serves as the slave flash. It should always be set on TTL mode and controlled by the Minolta system. Because the Mecablitz is controlled by weak flashes from the camera's flash unit, the ambient light should be as low as possible and the sensor of the SCA Adapter should be aimed at the main subject.

When using this combination, if the Minolta's lens aperture is changed, the Metz unit display will not be affected. The new aperture needs to be manually set on the Metz unit. Also, the flash unit's reflector is not automatically zoomed under all conditions, so you should set it manually to the widest (24mm) position.

Wireless TTL control is not the same for all Minolta cameras. On all camera models, wireless automatic exposure control must be set as advised in the instruction manual; then the camera takes over 1/3 of the illumination and the Metz unit supplies the larger proportion of 2/3.

Note: *The Maxxum/Dynax 9xi does not have a built-in flash unit, so wireless mode can only be used in conjunction with a Minolta flash control unit or a Minolta 5400HS or 5400xi flash unit.*

Painting with Light

The term "painting with light" refers to a flash technique in which one flash is moved to illuminate the subject from several positions. The photographer (or assistant) holds the wireless flash unit, moves to each position in turn, and fires the flash manually. Using this method you can light very big subjects that are too large to be adequately illuminated with a single flash unit. This technique is suitable for lighting up a meeting hall, factory, cave, or mine, and can also be used at night to illuminate buildings, bridges, etc.

To paint with light, place the camera on a tripod and set the shutter to B (bulb) or T (time). Fire the flash either manually at full power, or using automatic aperture mode. Automatic aperture mode is usually more suitable because it prevents overexposure of the subject. With the use of this technique, each flash illuminates a different part of the subject. When using this technique, take care that none of the flash is aimed at the camera lens. Also, do not include light sources such as streetlamps in the image area, because the long exposure times will allow them to overexpose the picture.

Increasing the Guide Number Using Multiple Flash

Many motionless subjects that do not require painting with light still require more than one flash for adequate illumination. This applies to subjects at a considerable distance, with lighting conditions are so poor that even a time exposure with the camera on a tripod does not guarantee perfect color reproduction, the ceiling of a dimly lit cathedral, for instance.

First, measure or estimate the distance to the subject, then multiply that by the desired f/stop to find the required guide number. For example, if the shooting distance is 36 feet (12 m) and you wish to use f/8, 36 feet x f/8 = GN 288. (Not even Metz offers a hand-held flash unit with such a guide number!)

Next, divide the desired guide number by your flash unit's actual guide number. With a desired GN of 288 and a flash unit with an actual GN of 96, the result would be 3.

Finally, square that number to find the number of required flashes, $3^2 = 9$.

$$(\text{Desired Guide Number} \ / \ \text{Actual Guide Number})^2$$
$$= \text{Number of Flashes}$$

$$= (288 / 96)^2 = 3^2 = 9$$

Rounded off, this means, for correct illumination of a subject at a distance of 36 feet (12 m) and an aperture of f/8, you should fire a total of 9 full-power flashes.

Bracketing exposures: To be on the safe side, make a bracketed series of exposures by firing the same number of flashes at f/5.6 and at f/11, as well as at the desired aperture of f/8. Since the flash unit needs time to recycle after each flash, the total exposure will take place over an extended period of time, so the camera should be mounted on a stable tripod and activated by cable or remote release. To avoid the effects of ambient light, instead of leaving the shutter open you can make multiple exposures, tripping the shutter separately each time but not advancing the film.

Allow for the fact that the flash readiness indicator will light up as soon as the flash has recycled to 70% of full power. To be sure of actually getting full power, wait for twice as long as it takes for the flash readiness indicator to light up. Using nine flashes at 70% power instead of 100% would require an additional four full-power flashes to achieve correct exposure.

Metz Flash Applications

Perfectly Lighted Portraits

Many amateur photographers dream of studio flash set-ups. Yet, by using several hand-held flash units, it is easy to create studio-like lighting. Several Metz flash units and the TTL Multiconnector SCA 305, or even two or three 40 MZ 2 units and wireless flash control, may be used easily and effectively and are much less expensive than an actual studio set-up.

Typical portrait lighting: In typical portrait lighting, one flash unit provides the main or key light. Professional photographers like to place the light at a distance of approximately 6 feet, positioned to one side of the camera or slightly above it, so that the center of the light is approximately 4 to 6 inches above the model's eyes. A small difference in the light's position, by just a few inches, can determine the quality of illumination.

Direct flash is not recommended for portraits. Light that is diffused by a soft box, umbrella or bounce card is usually more suitable.

Fill light for portraits: The basic rule is that the fill light should be half as bright as the main light, or less. This means that the telecomputer should indicate 1/2 stop less for the shadow areas than is set on the lens.

Catchlights: Particular attention must be paid to the highlights or catchlights in the subject's eyes. Each light source illuminating the subject's face from the front and side (up to a certain angle) creates a reflection in the eyes. The general rule for portrait photographers used to be that no more than one catchlight should show, of course, not many traditions are strictly followed today, modern portraits often have multiple catchlights.

Skilled portrait photographers also consider the appearance of the subject's eyes when setting up their lighting. Darker eyes, for example, are shown more effectively with soft illumination. Small

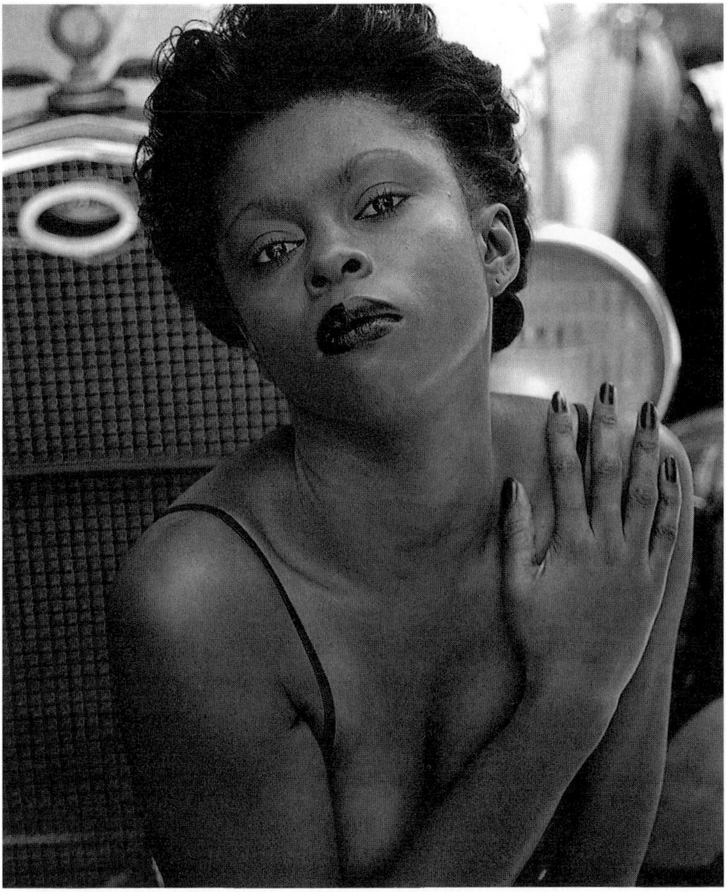

Using flash to supplement the ambient light increases the contrast and enhances details. Photo: Bob Shell.

eyes can be made to appear larger by positioning the lens slightly below the eye level, and deep-set eyes appear even more dramatic when the chin is raised slightly.

Highlighting hair: A hair light requires only a small flash unit, even older manual units will work well. The flash unit is set up behind the portrait subject and aimed to produce the narrowest

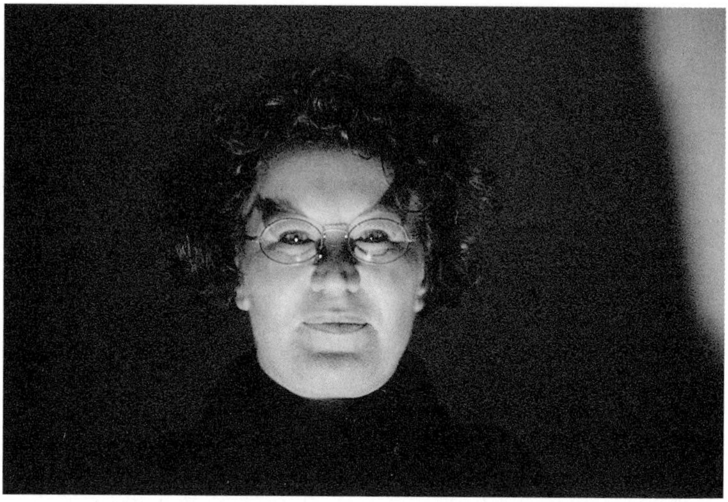

Although lighting the subject from below produces "demonic" results, it is sometimes suitable for theatrical photography and perfect for Halloween night!

possible light beam. This creates a subtle outline of the subject's hair. A gobo or other screen is useful to prevent any of light from straying into the lens and causing flare.

The background: Background lighting, like the hair light, is intended to separate people and objects from the background. Generally, for good separation between the subject and background, the background lighting should be one stop less than the lighting for the main subject. Placing more light on the background may result in over-illumination and poor separation from the subject.

Sometimes small "light islands" can be set up in the background by turning on existing room lamps or by using stronger incandescent lamps. Here again, consider the dramatic effects that can be obtained by creating shadows.

Alternative Lighting for Portraits

Two other types of lighting that should be tried by photographers making portraits are sidelighting and lighting from below.

Sidelighting: Sidelighting is always dramatic and can create an extreme brightness range. Sidelighting provides strong modeling for any surface because highlights and shadows show off every irregularity. The surface structure is enhanced, which is why some photographers call this "texturizing lighting." In portraits, sidelighting can dramatize the texture of the subject's skin. This is not always desirable, but works well for weather-beaten faces and wrinkles.

Sidelighting can also be used for dramatic effect, for example by lighting only half the face and leaving the other half in shadow. To add drama to this type of portrait, be sure the eye that is in shadow has a catchlight. The high contrast of sidelighting may challenge you to determine the correct exposure, but if the contrast is really excessive it can be reduced by using fill light.

Lighting from below: Because natural light does not come from beneath the subject, this method of lighting usually has an unnatural effect and should be used sparingly. One application would be to provide highly theatrical lighting for a portrait, to make the subject appear grotesque or even demonic.

Wedding Photography

Metz professional flash units are a standard among wedding photographers. This is due to the high power output, well-designed features and functions, and world-famous performance and reliability of a Metz Mecablitz flash. Wedding photography can be difficult and trying at times with lots of fast, changing action, pressure not to miss the "sentimental moments" and subjects who often are too preoccupied to cooperate much with the photographer. The last thing the photographer needs to be concerned with is the reliability and performance of his or her equipment.

Most weddings are shot with negative film and many professional wedding photographers are now using the new, faster films due to the advantages they offer and the improved grain structure.

Tricks for good flash results: Many wedding photographers use brackets such as those made by Stroboframe for natural-looking lighting plus flexibility in the fast-paced wedding environment.

(Also see pages 141-144.) These brackets raise the flash high over the lens to approximate natural light. This helps eliminate harsh shadows and red-eye, neither of which should be present in the proofs presented by a professional photographer. Portable flash diffusers such as those manufactured by Lumiquest are often used on the flash head to soften the light. Since modern TTL flash systems are a tremenduous advantage, Metz flash units can be used with flash brackets by taking advantage of the SCA connectors and adapters. Don't forget to compensate for the white wedding gown if it fills most of the frame in portraits of the bride. *(See appropriate sections in Chapter 2 and 4.)*

Fill flash is also an important technique for successful wedding photography. The best wedding photos almost always include a well-balanced, natural-looking touch of fill flash. Fill flash techniques are explained in detail in Chapter 4.

Large Subjects or Groups

Group shots are also a common subject in wedding photography. They are often shot under less than ideal circumstances with otherwise preoccupied members of the wedding party or various family groupings.

Manual flash: In full manual mode, the optimum exposure aperture for flash depends on the distance to the subject. In the case of a large group shot, keep in mind that every person in the group is at a different subject to camera distance, so even light coverage is always a consideration. This is often not much of a problem when the group is close together, but there are times, such as with a receiving line at a wedding, when you will have to pick a setting based on a middle distance between the beginning of the line near you and the end far from your position. This compromise is pretty much the best way to go, especially when you cannot arrange the group. If the light falloff is greater than one stop at the edges, then a decision should be made to take two pictures of a smaller area of the whole scene that are well lit, versus one that takes in the whole, but has significant shadow areas at the ends of the frame. Another consideration is the position of an important subject, such as the bride. The correct exposure should then be calculated around this person's position. This, then, becomes more a portrait of her on the receiving line as opposed to a group shot of the whole receiving line. One other possible solution is to use bounce flash off a white ceiling in this situation.

TTL flash: In TTL flash mode, the light reflected off the subject is measured even if the light is indirect. If the subjects are grouped close together or a bounce flash is used, TTL is the preferred approach. But in situations like the one mentioned above, TTL will react to the nearest subject whereas manual mode allows the photographer to control the exposure.

Variations in background illumination: Since scenes with a lot of depth tend to swallow flash illumination, ambient light can be used to balance the lighting by selecting a slow sync mode, depending on the camera model. In other words, use the flash at an aperture setting as close as possible to the ambient light to balance the light. This is only realistic and practical if there is enough ambient light to get within one and a half to two stops of the main flash illumination without having to resort to very slow shutter speeds which will record the blur of peoples' movement.

Flash for Interior Photography

When taking flash exposures, the photographer may select the lens focal length to determine the brightness gradient in a room. However, this does not change the ambient light in the room. And, because the flash is considerably brighter than any ambient room light, it is not necessary to switch off any light source. On the contrary, it might be sensible to switch on as many light sources as possible in order to create a clearly recognizable mood in the room. The short flash duration makes lamps recognizable as light sources but, at normal shutter speeds, they have no effect on overall illumination. In most homes this changes only when a picture is taken with a longer exposure time of 1/30 second or slower. However, one should always note that ambient room light will not be dominant; the light in a room will only be of importance when a picture is taken in existing light with just a touch of flash.

Copy Work

Lenses: As in macro photography, lenses that are optimized or appropriate for close-up work should be used when doing copy work. The best optics are those that have a flat field; that is, they are evenly corrected across their entire image area, as opposed to other lenses which are more likely to show a drop off in the center to edge sharpness and contrast.

Copy stand: A good copy stand is vital to keep the camera and the subject perfectly parallel and it is a good idea to use a bubble level to check the alignment of the camera relative to the baseboard when it is mounted.

Positioning light sources: Even illumination requires two lamps or flash units of the same power at an angle of 45 degrees to the subject set about 2.6 feet away from the subject on the baseboard.

Balancing the flash units: It is very important to make sure that both flash units are putting out the same amount of power to give even lighting. The easiest way to do this is to have units with the same power output, or whose output can be controlled in stops. It is also recommended that diffusers be used on the flash heads. Triggering can be performed via the SCA 305 Multiconnector cables. *(See page 149.)*

Still Lifes, Table Tops and Details

Many amateur photographers do not feel comfortable with taking pictures of still lifes and other subjects that require controlled lighting. In many cases, however, such photography can be done well in a light corner of a room or on a small table. The best approach is to work deliberately and gain some experience with simple subjects, by arranging the lighting in a planned way and studying its effects.

Edward Weston, one of the most famous of American photographers, is said to have developed his skill by experimenting with lighting on sweet peppers; today his best photographs of these are

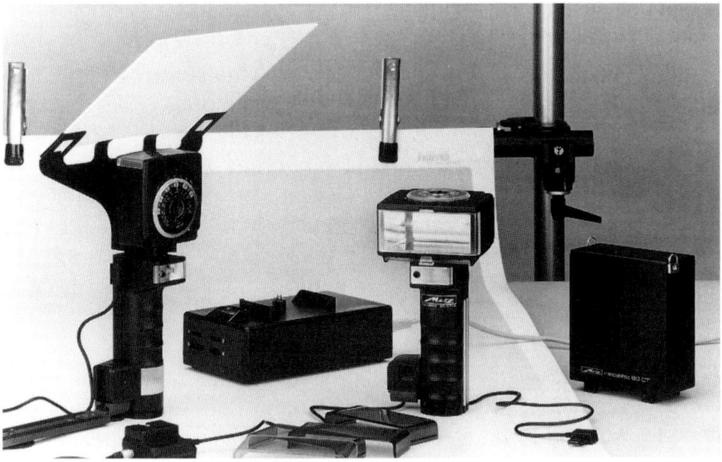

A couple of Metz handle-mount flash units in combination with some handy accessories become a compact yet powerful studio lighting set-up.

on display in prestigious museums. Irving Penn took hundreds of exposures of a white cup and saucer in order to see the most subtle nuances of light, to learn about them in order to utilize them later.

Flash connectors: Only techniques that have been mastered perfectly can be effortlessly applied to complex situations. Today, arranging perfect lighting for tabletop shots can be child's play by using the Metz TTL Multiconnector SCA 305 or wireless TTL remote flash control. *(See page 150.)*

Choosing backgrounds: Setting up a still life begins with selecting the background. Just as in portrait photography, the subject will stand out especially well from a background that is uniformly illuminated. A uniformly colored wall, a smooth cloth, or even a white or grey piece of cardboard offer the simplest solutions, and flash can be used to make these backdrops lighter or darker, or to add color.

Balancing the lighting: Again as in portrait photography, the lighting set-up starts with the main light. Often soft light is used to reduce harsh shadows, create broad rather than specular highlights and show fine nuances of color. If only one flash is used (at a 45 degree angle to the subject), place a reflector panel in line with the flash, behind the subject, and place another reflector at a 45 degree angle on the opposite side. Even softer light can be obtained by also using a softbox or other diffuser on the flash unit.

Adding a second or third flash should be done only after you have gained some experience with one light source directed at the subject (i.e., independent of background illumination). By using the TTL Multiconnector or wireless TTL remote flash control, this technique can even be applied outdoors.

Light tents: Photographing a highly reflective subject can be a real challenge. Tenting the subject is often helpful to prevent the camera, lights and other unwanted reflections from appearing. A light tent is simply a piece of light transmitting material which surrounds the subject and can be as simple as a piece of paper formed into a cone. A sturdier and more elaborate light tent can be made from rip-stop nylon or other sheer cloth draped over a simple wire frame. Cut a hole in the tent for the camera lens, and place several flash units around the tent to illuminate the interior evenly. If areas of the subject are too bright, place grey or black cardboard panels to darken these areas.

Close-up Flash Exposures

One of the most enjoyable and fascinating aspects of photography is making big pictures of little things. There is no other photographic field in which the advantages of electronic flash units are so obvious — daylight color quality, short exposure times, and small apertures.

Equipment for close-up photography: There are many lenses and accessories available specifically to make close-up photographs. The list includes:

Macro lenses
Close-up lenses
Extension tubes
Bellows

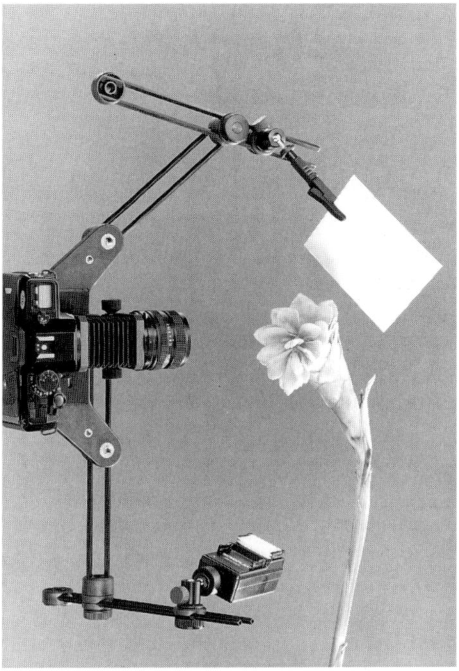

The Novoflex flash accessory line offers an impressive array of options for creative use of flash in close-up photography.

Teleconverters
Reversing rings
Magnifying filters
Macro flash brackets

Macro lenses have been known to be useful tools for many years. With these lenses the close-up range may be mastered easily, opening up a new world for many amateur photographers.

Most macro lenses have a maximum magnification of 1:1. Larger magnifications require more than just a macro lens. A bellows attachment can be used to extend the lens farther from the film plane for extreme close-up photographs, and will allow an already available lens to be used. Bellows units can also be combined with a macro lenses to expand their range even further.

Many photographers have the false notion that using bellows is complicated, tedious, and possible only with a tripod. While it is true that the very small depth of field in the close-up range requires a slightly slower and more careful adjustment of the focus, it is still possible to use a bellows attachment for handheld close-up photography. One secret is to preset the bellows for the desired scale of reproduction and then slowly move closer to the subject until it appears in focus in the viewfinder. This technique works well for close-ups at magnifications as large as 2X life-size.

Exposure compensation for bellows: Another reason photographers hesitate to get involved with bellows is the fear of exposure calculations. When the bellows is extended a distance greater than the focal length of the lens, an increase in exposure must be made. The formula for this is really quite simple: corrected aperture = normal aperture/(Image Scale + 1). If the subject on the film will be 1/2 its original size and the f/stop would be f/16 without the bellows, the formula becomes 16/(.5 + 1) = 16/1.5 = 10.6 or approximately f/11. Naturally, exposure compensation is not necessary when using TTL metering.

Flash position: The easiest method for making successful close-ups involves using a close-up setting and a close-up lens, with the flash unit mounted next to the camera or on one of the many macro brackets available such as those manufactured by Stroboframe. If the flash unit is mounted on the camera, take care that the flash is not aimed too high due to the parallax effect caused by the difference in height between the camera lens and the flash reflector. To avoid this problem, most Mecablitz flash units allow the flash head to be tilted down (below horizontal).

Reflectors: To be sure of lighting the entire close-up subject evenly, bounce the flash off a reflector. This also ensures that you will not be working closer than the flash unit's minimum flash distance. With an aperture of f/22, the minimum distance is the flash unit's guide number in centimeters. Another rule of thumb states that the minimum shooting distance is one-tenth of the maximum shooting distance. If the flash unit's display dial shows a maximum distance of 18 feet, the minimum distance between the flash and the subject should not be less than about 1.8 feet.

Problems with minimum flash distance can be solved by using the flash's zoom head at a wide-angle setting, by using a wide-angle attachment on the flash, or by lengthening the distance the flash travels via a reflecting surface.

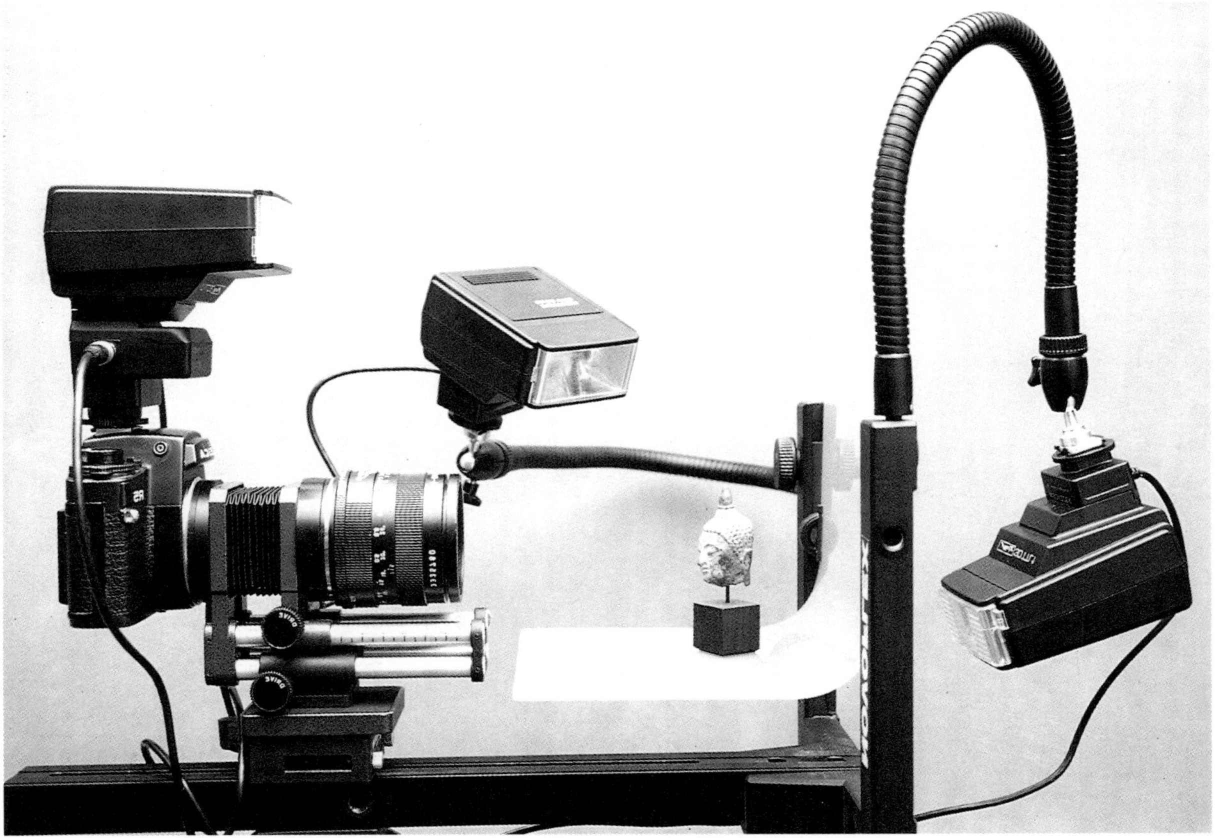

The Novoflex Macro S Copy Stand and accessories make photographing small products easy. Lighting is controlled from the camera by TTL flash metering and the use of the SCA 305 TTL Multiconnector.

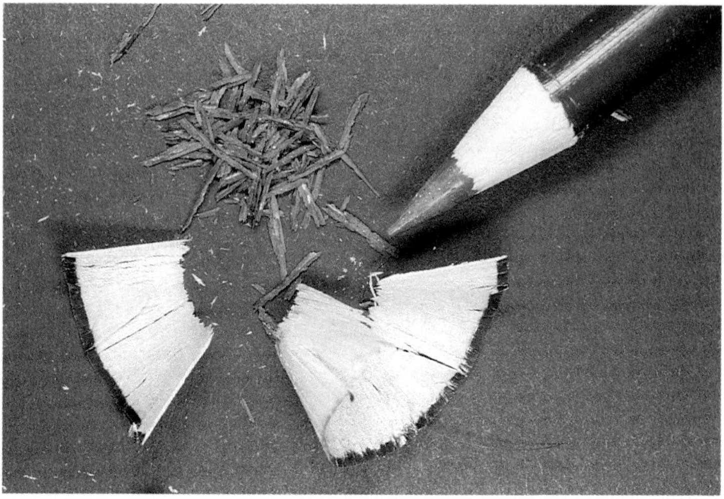

For extreme close-ups requiring a macro lens, extension tube or bellows unit, TTL metering will automatically adjust the flash for correct exposure.

Macro with TTL: If the camera provides TTL flash metering, no exposure computations are required and the exposure will be compensated for automatically. By using the zoom head in its widest position, the flash intensity will be somewhat modified. If the flash still proves to be too bright in test exposures, it may be attenuated additionally by means of a neutral density filter or simple white paper or tissue.

Depending on the film sensitivity, a minimum aperture is generally required for flash distances less than 25 inches. If a larger aperture is selected, the camera's TTL system may not have enough time to correctly adjust the flash.

Handheld macro flash photography: For handheld close-up photography outdoors, an excellent set-up is an on-camera flash unit (possibly attenuated by 1 stop with a light reducing filter) plus a second unit used off-camera, held by hand or with a special macro flash bracket. With this, perfectly lighted macro exposures at magnifications as high as 1:1 are possible. The second flash unit provides side light, adding a three-dimensional quality to pictures taken in sunlight (coming from the top) or with backlighting. TTL metering and the TTL Multiconnector SCA 305 make this technique very easy. Two or more Multiblitz 40 MZ 2 flash units are even more convenient because they offer wireless TTL metering.

Photographers who use a two light set-up like these will never want to return to the flat lighting provided by the circular ring-lights often used for close-ups.

Fill flash for close-ups: Close up nature photography often requires higher shutter speeds. A slight wind may cause a blade of grass that fills the viewfinder to appear blurred. A small amount of fill flash will sharpen the image of the grass blade. It also enhances colors; red poppies will look brilliant against a blue sky.

Short flash-to-subject distances can cause problems for TTL fill flash metering. A flash unit with a high guide number may not be able to shut off quickly enough, overexposing the subject. If you are not sure whether your flash can automatically cope with such short distances, use a reflector, neutral density filter or diffusion material to reduce the intensity of the light, and ensure that you are shooting within the working range of the flash unit and camera's TTL system.

Using a reflector will also soften the light and direct it downward, like natural daylight, thus eliminating light parallax and illumination errors.

Magic Lantern Guides

....take you beyond the camera's instruction manual.

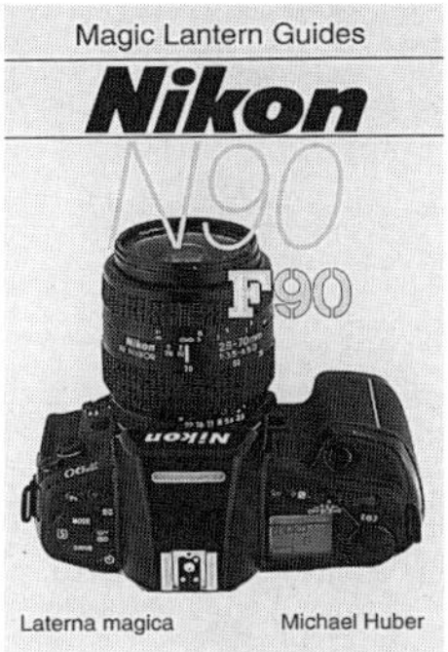

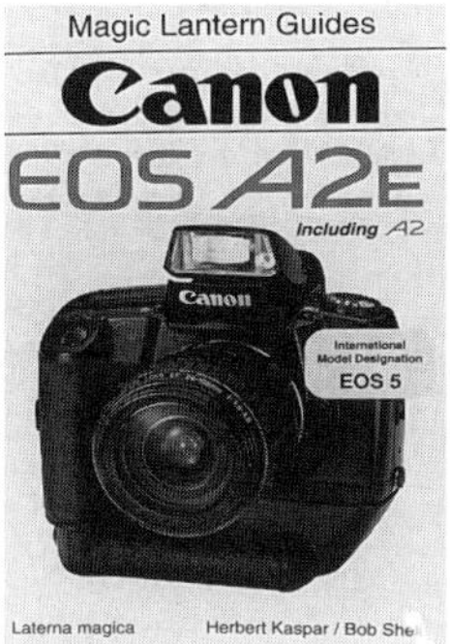

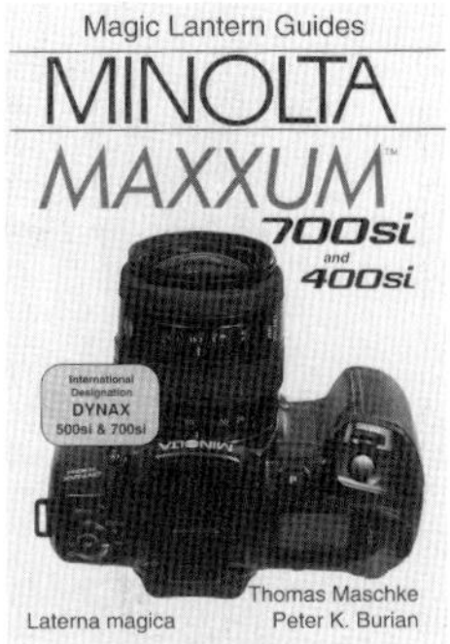

The world's most popular camera guides; available for most popular cameras.

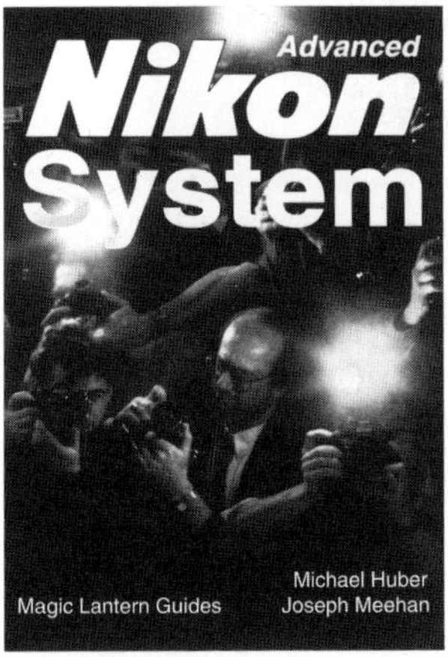

Magic Lantern Guide to the Advanced Nikon System
"I can't imagine a Nikon aficionado being without a copy of this book. It is essential equipment! Not only does it cover every Nikon camera likely to be of current interest to the serious photographer, it offers complete coverage of the all-important Nikkor lenses and accessories."
Bob Shell,
editor ***Shutterbug Magazine***

From Silver Pixel Press

Also by B. "Moose" Peterson. . .

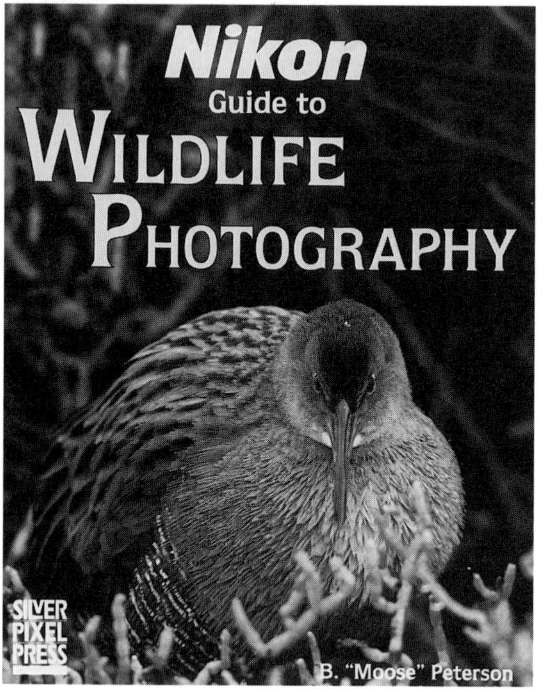

The Nikon Guide to Wildlife Photography
Ever wonder how the pros capture the stunning pictures we admire in the finest outdoor magazines? Is so, look no further than this new book by B. "Moose" Peterson.... Not merely another text on wildlife photography this book stands out among the competition because of three factors: extensive use of photos with detailed explanations, the significant emphasis on field ethics, and Peterson's explanation on how each species can be located, attracted or tracked... This is a virtual gold mine of information that will surely become an invaluable asset in increasing your success ratio of high impact images."
Peter K. Burian ***Outdoor Photographer*** *magazine.*

Notes